D0402982

Now That Our Kids Have Children

Grandparent's Prayer

Dear Heavenly Father—

I thank you daily for sharing with me the joys of children and grandchildren. Help me to be worthy as their parent on earth.

When I look at my grandchildren, I tend to exaggerate. Help me not to worship them nor even to idolize them. I acknowledge to you that although they are created in your image they are still human and have feet of clay.

Keep me also from holding on to my children and grandchildren. They really are your property, and I apologize for playing God to them at times, thinking that I have the right to tell them how to run their lives. Let me give advice sparingly, even when asked, lest I stand in the way of my children's growth as parents.

Help me to be both friend and helper to my children as they take on full responsibility as parents. Let me encourage and not criticize them; I know that judging is in your department.

Cause me to set such a good example in my life that my children and even my great grandchildren will be inspired to grow as persons as long as they live.

And help me to leave my longings for immortality in your care, not expecting my hopes and dreams to be lived out in those who follow me.

This is really all I have a right to ask but I wish you would help me to love them as you love all your children.

Amen.

Now That Our Kids Have Children

R. Lofton Hudson

WORD BOOKS
PUBLISHER
WACO, TEXAS

NOW THAT OUR KIDS HAVE CHILDREN

Copyright © 1981 by Word, Incorporated, Waco, Texas 76796
ISBN 0-8499-0305-X
Library of Congress catalog card number: 81-52522
Printed in the United States of America

Unless otherwise indicated, Scripture quotations are from the Revised Standard Version of the Bible, copyright 1946, 1952, © 1971, 1973 by the Division of Christian Education of the National Council of the Churches of Christ in the U.S.A. Scripture quotations identified KJV are from the King James Version of the Bible. Scripture quotations identified NEB are from *The New English Bible*, © 1961, 1970 The Delegates of the Oxford University Press and The Syndics of the Cambridge University Press. Scripture quotations identified TEV are from Today's English Version of the Bible, © American Bible Society 1966, 1971. 1976.

The quote on page 110 from *The Grandmother Conspiracy*, copyright 1974 by Lewis A. Coffin, is reprinted by permission of Capra Press, Santa Barbara.

To
My youngest grandchild
Zachary Hudson Hexum
Known to me as "Mr. Z."
Three years of age
"Unwept, unhonour'd, and unsung"
But never unnoticed

Contents

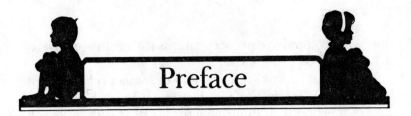

Preface

As Jessie, my wife (and since her retirement from teaching kindergarten a professional grandmother), read this manuscript, she said: "Is this written for grandparents or for their children?" The answer is, both. Whatever games are played between the generations requires understanding and participation on the part of both. It takes two to play games, so to deal with the interaction of three generations will require at least two of those generations becoming aware of what is happening. It is hoped that the third, the grandchildren, will benefit from smooth flowing communication and effective transactions between grandparents and their children.

One use of this little volume could be to pass it on to certain people who may pick up a few usable ideas from it. There may even be those who will mail it anonymously, like an Ann Landers column, hoping certain relatives will get the message—and they just might.

A better use, though, may be for parents and grandparents to read these chapters with an eye to avoiding obstacles in family interaction, and in keeping the relationships as free as possible from fear, resentment, coercion, and manipulation. The goals really are freedom, frankness, and feeling close.

If reading this book results in family members drawing closer to each other, then the author's purpose has been accomplished. After all, the words *family* and *familiar* are first cousins. Maybe the word *intimacy* has risen to the surface with full force in the last decade because our family life has suffered so severely from mobility, divorce, and

obsessive-compulsive preoccupations with getting and having, instead of being close.

To me, the heart of religion and of human relationships
is nearness. "He is not far from each one of us" (Acts
17:27). This book is about how to stay near without tread-
ing on each other's toes or getting in each other's way.

Please Release Them,
Let Them Go

THE POPULAR SONG, "Please Release Me, Let Me Go," could be the plaintive cry of millions of young people in the Western world.

They are asking to be adults, to be autonomous, to be individuals who stand as tall as their parents. It is not, as in the song, "I don't love you any more." Rather, the situation is more that they are saying, "I want to love and respect myself by making my own decisions, standing on my own feet, taking my own risks, being right or wrong in my own way." This is the only way anyone ever grows up. Even in very close-knit cultures, there are ways of initiating young people into adulthood. One way or another, children have to become adults. That is what we are aiming at as parents, to work ourselves out of a job.

At least some of us have been trying to work ourselves out of a job. If we do not let our children grow up, they suffer, we suffer, the grandchildren suffer. In fact, the sins of the parents get visited onto the children and grandchildren in a very real sense. Not because God does it, but because it is in the nature of faulty parenting. It is the sin of moms becoming manipulators and dads becoming dictators—the sin of parents becoming possessive.

Manipulators or Emancipators

The basis of all good grandparenting is the establishing of good relations with our children.

"Good" means workable, successful, respectful, and especially that which promotes the growth and happiness of all concerned.

By manipulation we mean that one person influences another to do what he/she wishes without concern for the self-direction and the conscious choices of the other. A manipulator prescribes the outcome. Often the hidden agenda—the unspoken assumptions—is the trick. The goal may be the satisfaction of the parent's power-hunger. It may be the perpetuation of a child-parent relationship so that the parent or parents will not have to face their own emptiness. The motives are varied and complex.

Often, parents consciously have the noblest of reasons for continuing to parent:

"I'm just trying to be helpful; you know that I love you both."

"I don't want you to have to go through what your mother and I suffered."

"After all, we have learned some things from the school of hard knocks; you can profit by these, we hope."

"We know what is best for you. Have we ever given you any bad advice?"

"Remember that we are your parents. We will always be. It will pay you to listen to us."

There are even parents who use the Bible to manipulate:

"Children, obey your parents," they quote. There is just one catch; the word for children is not just "offspring," but it's usually used about "little children." To say nothing about Jesus' plain directive about not calling anyone on earth your father, that we have one Father in heaven and all are brothers and sisters (Matt. 23:9). Because we all have the same heavenly Father, parents and their adult children are brothers and sisters—subject to the same authority. Their relationship is not to be one where the child submits unquestioningly to the parent's dictates, but rather an adult-adult relationship.

In other words, when children are little they have to be directed because they cannot direct themselves. Somewhere between childhood and the self-sustaining period of adulthood, children have to assume responsibility for themselves and their offspring (if any), and parents have to back off. This is well in line with what Jesus said to adults, "Call no man on earth your father." It means, as applied to the home, that when children grow up they should treat their parents like adults, and parents should treat their children like adults.

Nor does this adult-adult relationship between generations nullify Jesus' warning about mistreatment of parents in Mark 7:9–13. Both children and parents are emancipated, not manipulated, when undemanding love flows between them and only when their love is undemanding. Children—do not say, "I take no responsibility for your happiness or your security." Parents—do not say, "You are still my child, so I will tell you how to run your life."

HELP MANAGE THE MANIPULATORS

Adult children often overlook the fact that they are harming their parents when they allow themselves or their children to be manipulated. In the long run, by allowing this manipulation, they are contributing to the evil in the world.

Harming? Yes. They are contributing to their parents' deformation of character. They are allowing them to distort reality. They are helping them play God. They are stunting their growth and helping them settle down to practicing bad habits in relating to people.

That old saw about not being able to teach an old dog new tricks doesn't apply here. We are not discussing the interrelations in the dog family. Interdog behavior is no excuse for human self-defeating practices.

Here is what we are facing. Families go through stages which demand adaptive behavior on the part of each member. If these transitions are not made healthily, consciously, and sensibly, somebody gets into trouble. Unhappiness results. The stage is set for conflict, estrangement and hate.

In other words, when adolescents become adults and marry and start a family of their own, parents have to take their hands off, start trusting them and treating them like adults, respect their children's rights to make their own mistakes, express faith in the young people's ability to carve out their own niche in the world.

When parents try to play the let-me-help-you-run-your-life game, the game stops when children refuse to play it. It takes two to play any family game. When children say "no" to their parents' helpful overtures, the patronizing game ends. Then, or sometimes after a while, there will be a much better chance of an adult-adult relationship, which is what we are aiming for.

I cannot be too emphatic, however, in saying, "We don't help our parents by letting them tell us how to live our lives." We may remain the eternal child or they may keep up the self-defeating father-knows-best or ask-your-mother games. If they live long enough, the system must change. But even while they are in their "middle-escent" period, there are fewer hazards if adult-adult relations are fostered. They help us grow out of childhood. If necessary, we can help our parents make the transition into the next stage—the empty nest.

For example, how can we have the respect of our own children if we are letting our parents make decisions for us? Or how can our children learn how to handle us twenty years from now, if we do not insist on our parents treating us like adults?

LEARNING TO BE LIBERATED

There is another side to this manipulation-liberation struggle.

It is one thing to say, as I have, to children, "Don't let your parents manipulate you." But what of the child who maneuvers the parent? This is the other side of the coin.

I can think of four ways I have seen children maneuver their parents, sometimes to the devastating detriment of both.

1. *The guilt maneuver.*

The primary method of such children is to place the parent in a bad light as a parent. The formulation of the method starts with the words, "If you really love me." The implication is that you ought to show your parenting skills in a particular way. The blackmail aspect consists of the hidden threat which reads, "If you don't respond in a particular way, I will decide that you don't love me."

The payoff for the parent who responds in the expected manner is a good relationship, admiration from other relatives or the community, and the inner feeling of being a super-parent.

The payoff for the child and the in-law, is a built-in baby-sitter, money, free meals, a free savings and loan agency, a rescue squad on call, and a perennial Santa Claus.

The danger lies in the anger that almost invariably accompanies duress (or pressure) when parents are doing more than they wish, and in the child's unrealistic expectations which come from assuming that there will always be someone in the wings who will come to his rescue.

To avoid overt or covert anger on the part of both parents and children, then, we need to avoid making each other feel guilty. It is well known to psychologists that guilt and anger are closely connected. Guilt is on the surface, and anger lies close below the surface. So if parents make their children feel guilty, they will trigger anger. If children make their parents feel obligated and duty-bound, sooner or later, consciously or unconsciously, anger will follow.

2. *The need maneuver.*

Necessity is the mother of invention, so the proverb has it. Also, we may conclude, the needs of our children and especially our grandchildren are among the most powerful motivators of the over-forty man or woman.

Who can resist the temptation to give the grandson or the granddaughter the kind of lessons which will bring out those rare genius qualities which are so obvious to us, their grandparents? And, of course, we want them to have the best of travel, camping, health, and religious opportunities, to say nothing of clothes, toys, and transportation advantages. The need maneuver often takes the form of a subtle hint, such as:

"We would like so much for Johnny to go to camp this summer, but we cannot work it into our budget." Or "Sally is just dying to take violin lessons, and she seems so talented in music." Or "Andy's teeth could use braces; in fact, the dentist says they should be started at this age, but . . ."

Sometimes it is not even the parents who think of the dire need. One of the grandparents, or even some other relative may come to their aid and plead the grandchild's cause.

3. *The clan maneuver.*

One of the ways a young couple avoids freedom, perpetuates passivity, and dodges responsibility is by staying enmeshed in the family of one or both sets of parents and other relatives.

It is true that there needs to be a good word said for the extended family. Around the middle of this century, it looked as if relatives were becoming taboo. Now, with Alex Haley's book, *Roots*, and the interest it has generated in genealogies, we are probably growing in our appreciation of the maintenance of ties with blood and marital kinfolks.

However, maximum growth in the appreciation of family roots seems to come better and faster if the nuclear family develops its own ways of being independent and free. Even the communal family (several couples attaching to one another) did not seem to get off the ground. And the kibbutzim of modern Israel do not seem to be perpetuating themselves, according to the latest reports. It appears that blood probably is thicker than water.

It seems that the idea of knowing relatives, maintaining some kind of caring relationships with them, is advantageous. But leaning on relatives, depending on them to pull our chestnuts out of the fire, or running to them for advice or financial help often leads to cracking a marriage if not breaking it wide open. The clan just cannot be trusted to be objective. An in-law, after all, could be defined as a referee with an interest in one of the fighters.

A good rule for handling parents seems to be: love them but don't lean on them. And children need to avoid appealing to the clan instinct by soliciting help unless there is a dire need. It is better not to expect things just because you are kin.

4. *The meaning maneuver.*

Certainly, no one wants to destroy the happiness of another human being, any more than he or she wants to poison someone's pets or slash his tires. However, I have seen relatives—single people and childless couples—make a nuisance of themselves by trying to take over the children of their blood kin.

"He just loves me and gets so much out of being at my apartment."

"Why can't Sue spend the night with me? She always has such a good time."

These speeches, up to a point, are harmless. Beyond that, though, there is pressure, moral persuasion, and emotional coercion.

The clincher comes, though, when relatives, and especially grandparents, begin to insinuate that they can provide a better situation for the child than the parents can. These insinuations come in statements like: "Look how much I can do for them, and I do not have anyone else to love."

"How can you forbid them to spend the weekend with us, when you know how much it means to us?"

"You are so busy with other things; let us take this burden off of you for awhile. You know what it adds to our lives."

These helping relatives may put parents under duress. In any case, it is hard to keep the relationship pattern wholesome and clean. The fact is, many older people and some single people and childless couples ought to be more creative in finding their own happiness. If they are so open to helping the young, they might find it rewarding to seek out children who need foster parenting and foster grandparenting.

SOME CONCLUDING TRUISMS

For the rearing of children, it seems to be a good generalization that *the ones who bring children into the world are generally the best ones to bring up children in the world.*

In this day of the dual career family and fewer things (such as chores) for children to do, it is of value if relatives, neighbors, friends, and all who come into contact with children may make needed contributions to them. Most children and young people profit greatly and become better rounded human beings if they have intergenerational and interethnic and intercultural contacts. They are better prepared for the mobility which modern life often calls for repeatedly. How to effect these interactions between age groups, as well as other groups, is the problem we are facing in this book and in real life, but we must stand by the fact that parents are the ones to create and monitor these systems of interaction.

It will be observed by those who take a close look, however, that *children have the best chance of developing healthy attitudes toward living if they are reared by parents who have the independence and autonomy to make decisions without having to run to relatives for advice.*

All of us have been around people who turned us into big brother or big sister or Dutch uncle or parent. They have never learned to trust themselves to be parents, to risk being wrong in making adult decisions, and to have the courage to adventure into new paths of living and being. They either want to stay in the beaten paths or seek some guru as guide for them into the future.

A good rule of thumb for parents concerning children and grandchildren would seem to be: *Stand by them and stand out of their way; give little or no help until they prove that they can get along without it; then offer it only if they are free to reject it without feeling guilty or to accept it without feeling obligated.*

There is some good evidence, which could be obtained from any counselor's office files, that many parents find it more painful to give children up as they become adults than it was to bring them into the world.

There is a natural impulse—because of our patriarchal Western heritage and because of our deep-seated need to dominate the total environment—to hold on to our children, encouraging their dependency and adding stress to their marriages and insults to their egos.

Don't Tell Them
Unless They Ask You

ONE OF THE WORST habits relatives, including some parents, have developed is giving advice when no one asked them in the first place. Or to put it in the form of a rule: Never give advice unless it is asked for. This is the Golden Rule of interpersonal relations among relatives. Following it could be worth a fortune in peace and in avoiding uncivil wars among relatives.

"But they would never ask," one of my peers said. "Really," I replied, "then I guess you are stuck with teaching by example. Is that so bad? It may be the best way after all. You know the old saying, 'One example is worth a dozen precepts.'"

After all, one thing would certainly be accomplished. Relatives could let down their guards. All of us have heard someone say, "When that happened, I knew Mom would put in her two-cents' worth;" or "Dad never knows when to be quiet. When an issue comes up, he immediately starts out with, 'I'll tell you what I think.' The truth is, Dad has some good ideas, but he gives them so quickly and so dogmatically that everyone's teeth get on edge and they argue with him even when they would like to agree with him."

What's wrong with giving advice?

Perhaps we could see the problems more clearly if we ask why parents are so quick to give unasked-for advice.

THEY ARE IN THE HABIT

First, they are in the habit. When you were little they had to direct you, maneuver you, push you, pull you, stop you from doing things which might get you hurt. As you got older, you learned to ask permission, they learned to give directives. In the adolescent years you rebelled, and they laid down rules, and you asserted yourself—even in defiance of your better judgment at times. They lost some confidence in your ability to use good judgment and to assess reality properly.

Then you left home. During the last years of adolescence and the young adult years, especially before marriage, your parents asked you about your life, how you were doing. You reported without much reluctance, or you may even have welcomed talking over with your parents your job, your purchases, or your plans.

Then you married. Talking things over with your parents became a little more delicate.

As one woman said about her husband of two years, "Do you know that I discovered that every time he and I had a decision to make, before we had sat down to talk it over, he had already discussed it thoroughly with his mother and they had already arrived at a decision." Or a young man who had been married ten years said, "When Jan and I get in the middle of threshing out some problem she pipes up with, 'Why don't we talk this over with Daddy? He is always so wise;' and how do you think that makes me feel?" Another man told me, "Our marriage was headed straight for the rocks until I found out that my wife's divorced sister was coaching her at every point. She is a divorced social worker in the East and, looking back, I really believe she was trying to break up our marriage. Then I put a stop to my wife's talking over our problems with her sister."

Next comes the new day. A grandchild is born. We parents of the new young parents suddenly realize that our offspring have had no experience in rearing children. Our memory bank trots out some of our deposited and accumulated skills and wisdom. And we feel certain we can be helpful after remembering how inadequate we felt when first we faced the responsibilities of launching and steering a new young craft upon uncharted seas. Or were they uncharted? We have been over them. We can pass on some of our wisdom. Or can we? Well, let's try.

There we go, off to the races. We not only remember how we did it, but we fall back into the parent-child relationship with our grown child and the spouse. We volunteer out of the goodness of our hearts, out of our outdated experience, and from the center of our accumulated illusions about age and experience producing wisdom.

What happens to the new, and sometimes frustrated parents? They try to look appreciative. Or they half scowl in trying to hold in an emerging rebuke. Or they conform outwardly and try to apply the volunteered advice. But the fact remains that they did not ask your opinion or your directions, so they wonder how much farther you will go telling them how to manage their baby.

They Are So Much Wiser

Second, there is the illusion that middle-aged and older people fall victim to—the illusion that because they have lived through certain experiences, they are now authorities on how to handle them. They may even be falling back on the "wisdom" that their parents passed on to them.

It would seem that people have learned something by living on this earth. And that some infallible and transmittable wisdom has been accumulated by man. Surely we have grown wiser as we have grown older. "I would certainly not make the same mistakes if I were living my life over," we have said and heard said. Wouldn't we?

To me, it is downright puzzling that wisdom cannot be passed on from one generation to the next. Knowledge, facts of science, can. We build our present scientific understandings on the research of the past generation. But wisdom about how to live, how to get along with one another, how to find happiness, how to cope with life, seems to have to be learned all over by each newborn infant. Doesn't that seem strange?

I am convinced, however, that many of us who are over fifty or sixty years old are thoroughly sold on the idea that we have learned that special secret which could be taught to those who are to come after us. We must have learned something by rearing children. So why not pass it on to them fully developed, and save them from making our mistakes—assuming we made a few.

There are two basic and fatal mistakes in this reasoning. One, that we have learned something significantly valuable by our experiences. Two, already mentioned, that what we have learned is transmissible to our reasonable, intelligent, and grown children. I say "fatal" because that is precisely what unasked-for advice has been in many instances. Relations have been broken, great chasms have been created between people, feuds have been established between relatives, all starting with someone's giving unsolicited opinions. When will we ever learn?

I have seen parents who had trouble with their parents set the same stage with their children by trying to be helpful. In some cases, trying to save children from making serious mistakes with "our grandchildren." The Lord save us from the saviors!

Top-Dog, Underdog Mistake

The problem is, it seems, that when we start giving advice we walk into a role with our relatives which offends them. It is the top-dog, underdog role. Or in Transactional Analysis *(I'm OK, You're OK)* language, the critical parent speaks to the rebellious child.

When one adult comes on to another adult as if the first adult has the answers, the relationship gets in trouble. Communications specialists know that trouble arises between adults when one appears to hold one of three stances (1) "I'm smart and you are dumb"; (2) "I'm right and you are wrong"; (3) "I'm good and you are bad." These positions may have the form of "I'm spiritual" or "I'm experienced," or "I'm succesful," "I'm a good Bible student," "I'm the one who sacrificed to bring you into the world" (in the case of the parent), "I'm the one who is making the money," "I'm better educated," or "I've lived longer than you." Such stances become stumbling blocks between generations or between peers.

(Let's face it, most of us grandparents really are smarter than our children, even if they have been to graduate school or watched educational TV, but for heaven's sake let's not tip our hands.)

To have opinions is often to be opinionated. We have ways of saying that the parent pontificates (like right out of Rome), or is cocksure, or always thinks he or she is right. It is the I'm-right-and-you-are-wrong syndrome. No one is right all the time. Or, to put it differently, only God knows all the answers. When two adults get into a discussion, though one is twenty and the other fifty, it does not follow that either has the truth—the whole truth, that is. The hangup comes when one acts like he knows the one and true answer.

Good relations occur most often between people who treat each other as equals. They hardly ever occur, for long, when one acts like top-dog, whether the role is "Big Daddy," "Great Professor," the "Wise Granny," or "Doctor."

To put it another way, when Senior Citizens quit treating their children as "Junior Citizens," each looks the other in the eye, no one looks down on anyone, and one adult speaks to another adult as an adult, to the comfort of all.

It is a short step from playing parent to playing God. In fact, we are very much like God to our children when they are little. And when they get to be eighteen or twenty, somewhere along there, we need to stand on their eye level and assure them that they are not looked down on. Such eyeball-to-eyeball, equal-facing-equal communications will avoid many a toe-to-toe confrontation that leads to hurt and estrangement.

WAYS TO STAY ON EYE LEVEL

There are ways to keep your children on your eye level. When they were small they looked at your knees, then later at your tummy, then at your chin. Now they deserve to look you in your eyes as an equal, but it is up to you to help that happen.

Here are four rules which may help.

1. *At times just don't have an opinion.*

Shortly after our daughter married, she said to me one day, "Daddy, what do you think Terry and I ought to do about. . . ?" I cannot remember whether it was about a new car, going on to post-graduate work, where to go on a vacation, or what.

I replied simply and sincerely, "I don't have an opinion on that subject."

"Aw, come on, Daddy, you know you have an opinion. I'm not asking you to decide for us," she said.

I stuck to my guns: "I don't have an opinion. I don't

even plan to form an opinion on that subject. There are some subjects a couple needs to talk over with each other only. I don't have an opinion and I don't intend to, believe me."

She gave up. I guess they managed to make a decision without the old man's putting in his two-cents.

2. *Even if you have an opinion, point them to other sources for facts and information if that is advisable.*

Often your children will ask you questions about law, finance, medicine, electrical engineering, child rearing, or taxes when that is not your specialty at all. It may be smart to have them get more accurate facts from those who are experts, even if you have to pay for it.

If you tell them how to make out a budget, for example, it will likely be on the basis of your experience only, which may not fit their temperaments at all.

Or if you should tell them what others you know do, like about insurance policies, when to have children, or the relative value of renting or buying a residence, then leave it to them to double check with others and pool opinions. Otherwise, you may walk right into the trap of telling them what you think they should do and find that you are wasting your breath. This could lead to resentment on your part.

3. *When asked for your advice, stick to the question at hand.*

I know a couple who asked the wife's parents about the relative merits of buying a boat to be used on a nearby lake the coming summer. What they got was a lecture on the kind of expensive sports car the husband had already bought, the kind of clothes they both were buying, the inadvisability of accepting money from the other set of parents, and the relative merits of saving at least ten cents out of every dollar.

On the other hand, wise parents can often help their children weigh their options, look at their value systems, and examine their priorities. But only if they ask and if the parents can honestly say, "This is the way we look at it at our age, but hindsight may be working with us. We were not always so good with foresight. Don't let us decide for you; your judgment may be better for you at your age." But what parents can honestly make that speech? Some can.

4. *Give advice sparingly and humbly.*

I have already said, stick to the questions at hand. It is also important to avoid giving too much advice once the gate is opened for advice to pass through.

Think why advice so seldom works when parents dish it out. There are hardly ever two situations alike, considering the emotional and maturity levels of two different generations. Besides, if we are wrong, we may become the scapegoat (the one blamed) by inexperienced youth. Or if it does work, passivity and irresponsibility may be fostered by the very people (parents) who often complain loudly that young people today don't know what it is like to do without or to face hardship. It seems obvious, then, once we look at advice-giving, that to give it sparingly and humbly is most likely to get good long-term results.

In Chapter 1, I said that parents who know what they are doing are aiming at working themselves out of a job. Now we can add to that the following maxim: To promote the greatest amount of growth, self-reliance, and sound decision-making, we need to communicate to our children that they should learn to trust their own judgment and learn from their experience. The effectiveness of our communication shows best in what we refrain from doing, and sometimes in what we do sparingly.

Parents Obey
Your Children

IN THE NATURAL process of growing up the stage is set for confusion when parents have to shift gears as their children enter the teen years.

It is true that the Bible says, "Children, obey your parents." However, as I pointed out in Chapter 1, we often overlook the fact that the word translated *children* is used most often to refer to little children, not grown people who happen to be the offspring of two parents. If this applied to grownups, and they practiced full obedience as long as their parents lived, our society would be in trouble. We would never be able to scrape the barnacles off the ship of progress. Rebellion and defiance are necessary to forward movement in any culture.

My father back in the twenties used to say to me, "I hope you will be an improvement over your old daddy." He was not running himself down, for he was not a self-reproaching person. Rather, he was facing sensibly the fact that the world has to change, young people must reach out for new goals, each generation must try to surpass the former. "Our little systems have their day; They have their day and cease to be" (Alfred Tennyson).

There are inherent in human nature certain tendencies which have to be overcome if there is to be a successful transition from authoritarianism to new systems of interaction. To understand these is half the battle. The other half is allowing our children to make decisions on their own within specific episodes, and according to their own understandings.

WHY GEARS GRIND AS WE SHIFT

There has to be transition out of the obedience-dependency stage on the part of children and their parents. It's at this point that the gears are likely to grind.

Of course, children have to learn to cooperate, obey, conform, meet demands, and face up to the fact that all over the world people have to operate under authority systems. If children were born grown in body, with their tendency to be assertive and impulsive, there would be little likelihood of their ever being civilized. Instead, they are born small and must be toilet trained, taught to eat and sleep and play by rules, and oriented toward certain requirements of reality. Adults, parents, teachers, TV show producers, policemen, and church leaders—these all set limits, define reality, foster ideals, and aim at commitments (some to rules, some to principles, and some to persons and person-developed institutions). One way or another, we try to get the message across that there are some things more important than doing what you wish when you wish to do it.

Going through the little child period is necessary. Even moving into the teen stage of reexamining things for ourselves is valuable. It's at this time most of us hang question marks on what our authority figures present as the last word. Then we may move into a stage where we realize that there is no last word on most subjects, so we hold off writing the bottom line on most issues.

The gears grind, however, when other forces refuse to allow us to define issues for ourselves—when we're not allowed to determine what stars we consider worth hitching our wagons to. Some refuse to give us the right to decide whether or not we believe in the stars. We are stuck with our wagons and our gear-shifting motor vehicles. Who is to tell us what road to put them on?

Some parents are able to shift gears with their adolescents as they assert themselves. Some parents even admire them for having the courage to make up their own minds, and they tell them so.

On the other hand, some parents never admit that their children are grown. One man said to me, "Mom never will admit that I am grown; she still calls me her baby, but what can I do about it? My mother is strong minded." His wife said, "He could do what I did with my father. I told him that the next time he called me his little girl, I was gonna' give him a long vacation from me so that he could grow up. He never tried that 'little girl' gag on me again."

If parents do not shift gears successfully, their children face difficult problems which will, consequently, affect grandchildren, and everybody's happiness and healthy interaction is marred.

The Mutual Shifting of Gears

The trick in family interaction is for the gear shifting to occur simultaneously.

It sometimes occurs when a child goes away from home, to college or to distant employment.

A mother wanted to caution her son as he left for college: "Now Sammy, I hope you will not go to that college and out of loneliness jump right into a love affair and up and get married before you finish college. Remember, we have put a lot into you and are expecting a lot from you. There will be plenty of time to get married later." As soon as she paused to grab a breath, Sam said: "Aw, Mom, where do you get crazy ideas like that about my getting married? Not from me! How could I get married? I'm not divorced from you yet."

The emotional distancing that contributes to the autonomy of parents and children alike requires someone to be strong enough to take a stand. Not always, of course. Sometimes I see a family that seems wise enough to make the transition without too much turmoil and who can tolerate the appropriate grief.

It has been my experience with thousands of counselees, many friends and acquaintances, and in my own family life, that there are usually some rough times in this distancing period. I prefer not to call it separation anxiety because, if it is handled well, separation need not be a part of the scene. Instead, it's only a time of emotional distancing. The appropriate and usual experience is grief. If people do not know how to grieve healthily, consciously, and unashamedly, the emotion will come through as anger (which is often a part of grief). But whatever the conscious emotion, it need not be catastrophic to the relationship.

When either parents or children do not understand the importance of distancing or the importance of experiencing independence of each other, then one of them will usually have to take a stand. Often the other gets hurt; sometimes both suffer traumas.

This is illustrated by the story of the woman who, upon the occasion of the first fight with her new husband, phoned her father crying, and recounted the fact that Jimmy was neglecting her, that she was lonesome and disgusted. . . . The wise father heard her out, reasoned with her gently, and finally realized that she was merely putting on a campaign to get her own way as she had done so many times as she grew up. He realized that someone had to take a stand and set the stage for her growth. At last she came to the punch line: "Daddy, can I come home, move back?" The father knew that this had to be the moment of decision. Before he hung up the phone, he replied quietly but firmly: "My dear, you are at home."

One can imagine the daughter's burst of childish fury, but she got the message. The father had put off confronting her with painful reality too long already. He acted in a manner that seemed cruel but turned out to be setting the stage for a needed transition into adulthood.

Now assuming that two young people have learned how to leave their parents and be joined to each other, as both Testaments and thousands of years of tradition have taught, they move, then, to the next gear shifting phase and, then, to the next. These continued passages from one period to the other are often overlooked. Sociologists have delineated the empty nest period and the importance of the child-launching process. Next comes the restructuring of the leadership patterns involved when we move from one stage to another in our interrelations with our extended families.

The New Acknowledged Leaders

The crux of the problems in the newly established families, especially in relation to previous attachment systems, is that of who is the leader. Or who are the leaders?

The use of the word *obey* hangs on in our culture in spite of our professed democratic ways of relating. It arose, of course, in the days when the king-subject and the master-slave formats or metaphors were primary. Subjects had to submit to the authority of their kings. Slaves were beaten if they did not obey their masters. In the Hebrew culture, as judged by many passages in the Book of Proverbs about sparing the rod, using the rod of correction, beating the child with the rod (e.g., 13:24; 22:15; 23:13–14), we may assume that they really believed in the non-biblical phrase, "spare the rod and spoil the child."

What God, however, and all parents and wise grandparents want from those under their leadership is cooperation—willing, free, loving cooperation. Jesus said it clearly in John 14:23 that if we love him, we will keep his commandments. And he preferred to think of his disciples as friends, not as servants in a master-slave relationship (John 15:15).

In spite of these important insights, we still find parents who want unquestioned obedience from their children as long as they (the parents) live. They think that they are fostering a system of authority which will counteract the excessive and impulsive freedom of our day. The fact is, though, they have the same misunderstanding of the Old Testament which characterized the Pharisees of Jesus' day. Their "chain of command" system of family life turns away from grace and submits to the bondage of the law.

Precisely, the problem is, who is the leader? Whatever the method of discipline, the lifestyles of the new generation of children, the language patterns they are allowed to follow, their eating or sleep habits, we have pretty well arrived at the day when we can agree that whoever brings children into the world should bring them up in the world. There are exceptions, of course, such as baby-sitters, foster parents, and whoever has the care of children at times, such as grandparents.

But the question of acknowleged leadership is important. The leadership does not reside in those who are older and have more experience, nor in child psychologists, nor in the government or courts (except in extreme deviation from rules, as in child abuse). It resides in the natural or legal parents of the child.

It's important for all concerned—the grandchildren,

their parents and the grandparents—to acknowledge the source of leadership.

If children do not know who the final authority is, they may pit their parents against their grandparents, or vice versa.

If grandparents do not accept the authority of the parents, they may consort with their grandchildren to avoid the rules and regulations of their parents. Thus, they (the grandparents) contribute to the distortion of reality and to the development of faulty consciences in their grandchildren. All psychologists agree that young children, particularly, need a consistent pattern to follow in their learning what is approved and what is disapproved behavior. It is best if school, church, community leaders, parents, grandparents, and other relatives offer essentially the same values, foster the same rules, and set the same examples. This, of course, is never entirely possible in a pluralistic culture such as ours. The next best plan, then, is for those who are in the recognized kinship group to offer consistent leadership and example to children. This particularly applies to grandparents because children tend to revere them next to their own parents, and sometimes above their own parents.

PARENTS OBEY YOUR CHILDREN

Since the leadership of children is the primary responsibility of their own parents, grandparents should respect both the rights and obligations of the parents and help maintain their image as leaders. In other words, grandchildren should be treated as their parents say.

Parents obey your children—accept, acknowledge, and foster their leadership as the parents of your grandchildren. It's better, of course, when cooperation is voluntary and based on respect for the wisdom of the parent. However, during adolescence children often need to be encouraged to accept their parents' leadership because this is the only realistic way to avoid confusion and anarchy in the home and community.

I can think of five important areas where the parents' leadership should be carefully followed by grandparents. These are not all of the problem areas between three generations, but they illustrate the principles that may apply to all others as well. And they demonstrate the value of obeying your children.

1. *Eating and sleeping habits.*

Here's how not to do it.

Grandma picked up the children on Friday evening after school so that Sue and Charlie, their parents and grandma's and grandpa's children, could get away for the weekend.

Grandma said to her daughter-in-law, "Now I want to keep up their habits like you want it done, so tell me exactly what you have in mind for bedtime, what to eat, and any instructions about the way you want them cared for." Sue was grateful for her mother-in-law's consideration. She was explicit. What she did not anticipate was bull-headed Grandpa, her father-in-law.

Alice (twelve) and Dan (ten) were no trouble. They were smart enough to know that if they did not cooperate they would not be allowed a return engagement at the grandparents' house. There was some hassling over whether or not they could start seeing the late show. "Just let us see one hour of it." Gramp couldn't see anything wrong with making an exception, but Grandma won. They went to bed on schedule.

Dick (seven) was another matter. He had asthma and was allergic to milk products. Gramp thought this was a lot of poppycock. Allergies were all in your mind, he claimed. So at the Saturday afternoon circus he bought Dick an Eskimo pie. That did it. The attack of asthma sent them to the emergency room of the local hospital.

The doctor could not risk treating him without the parents' consent. Long distance calls had to be made to the parents at the lake. Fortunately, they could be reached.

"Dad, how could you be so stupid?" Charlie said. "Next time we will write it down on paper for you."

All of this because Grandpa would not obey, or cooperate, or acknowledge the leadership of the parents.

2. *Dress and baths and hair.*

At various periods in a child's life clothes become a major issue. They will sometimes try to draw one or both grandparents into the controversy, like, "Dad thinks this dress is too short, Granny; do you see anything wrong with it?" The only answer to such inquiries is, "I'm not in this. I do not have an opinion. When your mother was your age, your grandfather and I made such decisions. Right or wrong, we decided. Ask your parents."

And very few little boys want to take baths. Some, depending on what they have been doing, do not need a bath every night. Families differ. If the grandparents do not know the parents' protocol, they should ask.

Sometimes the parents' leadership can be damaged by a question like, "Does your father know that you have that on?" Or, "When did you get a haircut last?"

I know one grandparent who made the management of haircuts doubly difficult for the parents by saying, "I don't want Jack back in my house until he gets his hair cut." Jack was fourteen and about ready to get his hair cut, or at least styled. But upon hearing the ultimatum of his narrow-minded grandfather, as he called him, he showed his strength by defying two generations at once. When his parents pressured him, he threatened to run away from home. The least his grandparents could have done would have been to remain neutral.

3. *Money matters.*

Problems here range all the way from giving a small grandchild pennies or nickels, or silver dollars, to the setting up of trusts to become the property of the youngster at eighteen. The hazards are many.

In the first place the importance of money as rewards, or bribes, is questionable as a means of motivation. Money should be a reward for services, not a buying of love nor a bribe for good behavior. Grandparents should not be looked upon as money trees, or as perennial Santa Clauses, or as soft touches when children cannot wrangle money from their parents.

Again, the principle involved is "parents, obey your children" in certain matters.

If parents wish Grandma to have her cornucopian bag full of surprises every time she arrives, with an appropriate gift for each child, and Grandma wishes to play that game, I see no objection.

Or if Grandpa feels better by passing on brand new dollar bills, old coins, or bonds for birthdays, and the parents can integrate this into their training children in good money values, who is to object?

But suppose son, or daughter, or both, say: "Mom, Dad, we feel that our children are getting the idea that we cannot make a living for our family, so would you mind refraining from gifts for now?" This is where perception and imagination and empathy come into play. Grandparents need to say, "We're glad you can be frank with us about this. You are the ones to make that decision. Would it be better if we slipped the money to you and never let the kids know that it came from us?"

Parents, obey your children concerning the money you wish to give grandkids.

4. *Visiting and trips.*

"How would you like to go home with us, Johnny?" can set off a chain reaction. Of course, he wants to go, anywhere. *Go* is a magic word to most kids. It is "open sesame" to something novel and exciting.

Another is: "We're going to Jamaica in July this summer.

How about taking our grandkids with us?" The grandkids are sitting there listening. How could any but the most selfish and mean parents keep them from having a wonderful time on the beaches of Jamaica? So the stage is set for conflict and misunderstanding between children and their parents, and between their parents and their grandparents.

A little tact and strategy might have avoided the whole angry scenario.

For example, at the time I am writing this, my wife and I have been invited to be two of the leaders on an educational tour this summer, a fourteen-day Scandinavian cruise. We would like to take along two of our grandchildren, a boy, eight, and a girl, ten. Did we ask them directly? Not on your life. We do not enjoy a civil war.

We asked their parents. They thought it over and said that they would bring it up to the kids on Christmas Day, a sort of added surprise for the season. The kids agreed, in fact they jumped at the opportunity. I will tell you in my next book whether it was a treat for all of us or whether we laid the foundations for World War III.

5. *Religion.*

I knew a couple who got along beautifully in a "mixed religions" marriage until the first baby was born. He was a Baptist and she, a Roman Catholic.

When little Nancy Ann came, her maternal grandmother sent a christening dress and said to let them know when they were to have the Sacrament of Baptism. They had not planned to have the baby christened. The father objected to infant baptism. The mother was a lukewarm Catholic. Now that the issue was on the table, something had to be decided. After several long-distance calls, an exchange of letters, some weeks of coldness and estrangement, the young couple decided to go through with the christening. But today they are both active Presbyterians.

On one occasion my wife, Jessie, tried to sneak in a

little religion on our then three-year-old granddaughter, Angie. We were on a delightful vacation motor trip in Canada and had arrived at our motor inn about dusk. We had eaten and my wife and little Angie were sitting out on the beautiful back lawn of the motel in a swing. The temperature was perfect.

And the almost-full August moon seemed to hang about 200 feet above and beyond the small lake. As the two of them were looking at it, Jessie, who had been worried a little because our children were not taking our grand-daughter to church as much as Jessie thought they should, proceeded to say:

> I see the moon and the moon sees me
> God bless the moon and God bless me.

Then she went on to say, "Angie, do you know that God loves you?" After a brief pause Angie said simply, "Damn."

Jessie doesn't remember what she did or said for the next few minutes. In wars they call this shell shock, I think. She supposed that she said something about how God who made the moon and every other thing in the world loves each one of us.

Later, in recounting the event in private to our daughter and son-in-law, it became evident that Angie had heard one of their guests, a man, use the word *damn* over and over, even when talking about good and delightful things. To listening little Angie, it was a good, enjoyable expletive, or at least a word with no stigma attached.

Whether sneaked in or by direct confrontation, up to a certain age, grandparents must face the fact that parents have the right to say what their children are subjected to religiously. Many parents today fear the religious brain-washing of certain groups, whether by sects or atheists or by evangelical Catholics or Protestants.

On the other hand, many parents welcome the help of

their parents in transmitting to their offspring the values of faith and in leading their children to identify with a Power that will enable them to reach toward their potential.

In any case, the principle of acknowledged leadership holds equally in all matters of religion. Right or wrong, wise or stupid, pagan or Christian, agnostic or devout believers, the parents have the right to say what their children are to be subjected to.

Grandparents have the same opportunities all other good people have: be a beautiful person and you will attract others. Young people are looking for models. If you are a beautiful Christian, sooner or later they will be asking you how you got that way. Then you can witness in freedom and sincerity to what Christ means to you.

Don't Sabotage
Authority

GRANDPARENTS ARE USUALLY pictured as soft, sentimental, and sacrificial. This, of course, does not apply to all grandparents.

Many are self-centered, sour, severe, and somber. *Austere* is the word one of my British friends used about her grandfather. This ilk is impatient and critical and should be shielded from children. They can poison and damage children. About the only good the fussy and overdemanding grandparent can do for his or her grandchildren is to give them an exorbitant appreciation for their parents. For example, a grandchild says, "Mom, I don't know how you turned out so good when your parents are like they are." About the best thing that can be done for the grandchildren of the crabby, critical grandparents is to keep them away from their grandparents as much as possible.

This is not always possible, especially in connection with

broken homes. A grandchild may come under the toxic (poisonous) influence of such a grandparent because the choice is between him/her or them or a disinterested baby-sitter. Sometimes economic considerations put the vulnerable child and the severe grandparent together. In this case, the child should be coached in developing coping devices and transcending systems for not letting his/her grandparents cause them to be bitter, rebellious, cynical, or whatever the tendency is in such a toxic environment. Neither parents nor grandparents can ruin a child, as shown by millions of people who have risen above terrible backgrounds. But somebody usually has to tell them how to overcome these experiences.

The majority of grandparents, I am convinced, will do everything they can not to undermine the authority of their children with their grandchildren. They have observed through long years of experience the tragic mistakes of overpermissive parents. They have seen the crippled lives of children who did not learn to be reliable and responsible. They see the danger of severity as well as the tragedy of softness and refusal to face reality. They may flinch when their grandchild is struck by their child, they may hurt when the grandchild cries or complains loudly of unfairness or deprivation, but they know from personal experience and observation, that the authority of parents must be maintained. A good slogan to give a young child is: Your parents may not always be right, but they are always your parents. Grandparents must come in second as authority figures.

Somebody Has to Call the Shots

When we are young and economically dependent, the authority lies in those who feed and clothe us. When my father said to me at fifteen, "Young man, when you get to where you don't wish to obey me, you don't put your feet under my table." I had a pretty good idea which table he meant. He also knew my proclivity for eating.

Before that time, and after, however, I had come to understand some other kinds of authority. In school and in church I realized that certain people could say "Do this" and "Don't do that," even if they had to call my parents for backup support. When I drove a car, I realized before long that there were authority figures around. Even when I was standing around the stove in a country store or near the counter of a larger store in town, making a purchase, there was an invisible law relating to "property rights," backed up by authority figures called policemen and sheriffs.

Before long I began to understand that there were dimensions of behavior which came under the head of moral laws and natural laws. This came to mean that life and nature were made a certain way, and if we moved at cross purposes to these laws, we might get hurt or punished or even killed. Somewhere along the road of the discovery of moral and scientific laws, I came to the painful realization that I was responsible for my own behavior, even if no one were looking and if they should never find out. This, along with a reasonable and healthy self-respect, led me to formulate some of my own goals and convictions, only to revise them a hundred times since.

AUTHORITY HANG-UPS

The problems arise, inter-generationally, when families get hung-up on what or who is authority and how to arrive at procedure under a given set of circumstances. Value systems and who is to administer the system—who has the final word on the subject—get right in the middle of authority hang-ups. Here are the main examples:

"Thus saith the Lord." This is the most common authority base for religious people, at least those who belong
to Christian communities. The same is somewhat true for
Muslim and Jewish groups.

Christians fall roughly into two groups, so far as authority is concerned. Those who, in one fashion or another,
go directly to the Bible for their authority and reserve
the right to interpret for themselves what "the Word"
means. They may say with Alexander Campbell, "We
speak where the Bible speaks and are silent where
the Bible is silent." This is rarely true, however. They
usually mean, "We quote a verse of Scripture where one
clearly applies, and we find a vague one and make it
apply when we want to make out a good case for something."

It is well known to Bible students that people find verses
that will prove their point when they are gung-ho on proving a point. They found verses to justify slavery, to stop
women from cutting their hair, to keep blacks from having
their full rights, and now verses to keep women from being
preachers and deacons.

If you don't agree with their use of the Scripture, they
will question your sincerity, your spirituality, your sensibil-
ity, or even your political affiliation. Grandparents who
use this approach can create many problems for their offspring and their grandchildren.

I have seen divorced persons who were practically cruci-
fied by some authoritative figure, usually a parent, saying:
"You know divorce is wrong; you can never marry again
according to the Bible;" or "Just look at what it will do
to the children." These are exceptions these days. Most
Christians are coming to understand the meaning of grace
and forgiveness, rising above legalism, and realizing that
in God's sight divorced Christians are not second-rate
Christians.

"The Bible Teaches" Hang-up

This is not to say that the Bible is not a useful guide and norm. In fact, there is a return to "the Book" now as at no other time since the Reformation and the invention of printing.

It does mean, however, that when someone blandly or loudly says "The Bible teaches" or "The Word of God says," we need to begin asking some basic questions such as: Where does it say that? To whom was it spoken or written? How do we know it applies to the issue at hand today? Are we making the New Testament into a set of laws or rules (legalism) as the Pharisees did the Old Testament and the traditions in Jesus' day?

Those who quote Mother Church or Holy Bible are usually getting around to telling someone that he/she is sinning if he/she does not do this or that according to their interpretation. Therefore, if we do not ask serious questions about who is interpreting the Bible in a certain way, people will lay on us their rigidities and irrationalities and completely forget that there are alternate ways of looking at a particular interpretation. Thereby they prove that a woman ought to behave exactly as she did in the first century, that x number of church services a week are required by God, and that blood transfusions are contrary to the will of God.

Authority as Tradition

Very closely associated with—and similar in spirit to—the "It's in the Book" approach is "the Church teaches." From the way it works out in every-day transactions, it doesn't matter much whether we say, "Mother Church says" or "the Bible teaches." If we are determined to hold to an unexamined background of rules and regulations, we will find ways to pin down ideas and put a halo of authority and sacredness around them.

For example, from the Puritan days on, until this century when John Dewey, John Watson, and Dr. Spock and a few others had their influence, "spare the rod and spoil the child" was considered a valid maxim for child rearing. In fact most people thought it came from the Bible and was God's truth. I bet my mother twenty dollars once, after I had attended the seminary, that the "spare the rod and spoil the child" expression was not in the Bible. I think she died looking for it, back in the fifties.

The fact is, that quotation is from Samuel Butler's *Hudibras,* published in the seventeenth century. A Greek dramatist by the name of Menander who lived about 300 B.C., wrote: "The man who has never been flogged has never been taught." The writer of Proverbs wrote, "He that spareth his rod hateth his son: but he that loveth him chasteneth him betimes" (13:24, KJV).

Yet, research over the last fifty years has shown that there is a direct correlation between a parent's beating a child and the child's beating up on other children. As an adult, the same child is, himself, often guilty of spouse abuse and child abuse. Violence in the family is contagious. Now, in the last decade we have turned up not only child abuse and spouse abuse, but "granny slamming" and "gramp abuse," all springing from the same beating patterns in childhood.

Yet would you believe that in 1979 I heard over a Christian broadcasting station a powerful plea for rearing children by the rod. His text was Proverbs 22:15: "Foolishness is bound in the heart of a child; but the rod of correction shall drive it far from him." If he had looked closer, he could have found a verse that said that if a son will not obey the voice of his mother and father and is "stubborn and rebellious" that the men of the city, the elders, "shall stone him with stones, that he die." This shows how an uninterpreted authoritarian system simply has no relevance to our modern, democratic, love-as-a-motivating-factor home.

REASONS FOR CHANGE

I labor this point for three reasons. First, we are living in a frightening period in history when millions of people are looking for pat, pinned-down, black and white answers—simple answers to complex problems. So they rush to the conclusion that the Bible has the complete answers; it must have the answer to how to rear children as well as how to become children of God. Not so. The drug problems, or tobacco use, or unchaperoned dating, or how long children are to be considered children, or what age is the appropriate age for marriage, or what training is needed for life vocations—none of these are addressed in the Bible.

And even when we depend on the tradition in our culture, like a person's being free to marry when he, or he and she, can make a living, we must keep changing in the light of the changing times. Change is not only inevitable, it is desirable. Unless we think by some preposterous presumption that we are already full-grown Christians in the best of all possible worlds.

Second, I have seen over and over that when religious parents wish to dominate their children in prescribing how their grandchildren are to be reared, they appeal to religion using such statements as, "You know that is against God to let them do that on Sunday."

"My daddy always said, 'Show me how you treat your parents and I'll show you how your children will treat you.' "

"Think what you are doing to our grandchildren by your example; you know the Bible says the parents' sins will be visited on the children."

"You know the father is head of the house according to the Bible, if he doesn't assume the spiritual leadership, God will punish all of you."

I have heard all of these said by otherwise bright people, and even said to grandchildren and in front of grandchildren. It not only assumes a know-it-all attitude, but tends to undermine the much needed authority of two frustrated parents who have enough problems without grandparents butting in.

Third, the only way on earth that the parents of children can be real leaders with authority in their family is for grandparents on both sides to stay out of authority roles. Just do not assert yourself unless you are asked to or unless there is an extreme situation like child abuse, sexual molestation, or some condition which may require legal action. These are rare. And when they occur, it is rare that grandparents are the ones who can intervene.

Parents need to be free to be proper parents. This, of course, also means freedom to make mistakes. So grandparents must learn to hold their peace even when the parent's behavior seems improper to them, whether it's taking a child out of the grocery store and spanking his behind, or grounding a teenager for a longer period than seems reasonable or scolding in a way that may seem too loud or harsh. The list could go on and on.

But there will be far less damage to the child who gets some severe handling by a parent than there will be from an interfering grandparent. When grandpa or grandma breaks in on a dialogue between a parent and child, and reprimands the parent, or tries to modify the parent's directive, he/she is saying to the grandchild, "Your parents are often wrong and you do not have to obey them; they are unreasonable so get around it if you can." This is damaging to character. It is true that the parent is often wrong. There are no perfect parents. But as long as you live, on this planet, there is some authority that has to be obeyed. When you are small it is your parents and parent figures (teachers, policemen, neighbors when they are in their yards, etc.).

That is why the expression "Of course I spoil my grandchildren; that's what grandparents are for" is so utterly stupid. It is unrealistic, misguided, unscientific, unchristian, and harmful to the grandchildren. It may be detrimental to the parents and their relationship with their own children. It certainly is confusing to children.

AN ILLUSTRATION

Let me illustrate. And, of course, this does not mean that my wife and I are perfect grandparents, not by a long shot. In fact, right now I feel more inadequate as a grandparent than I did a month ago.

We have just returned from an eighteen day vacation in England. It was a month before the Royal Wedding. The parents lent two of their three children to us for this trip, you might say. Angela is now thirteen and Nicholas is eleven.

Last year and the year before that we went on Eastern Airlines Unlimited Mileage Vacation. We covered in the two years Barbados twice, Disney World in Orlando, Mexico City once, Cozumel and Cancun on the Yucatan peninsula, Houston, Atlanta, New Orleans, and New York City.

Four years ago, when they were eight and ten we went on a Scandanavian cruise, on which I was speaking, to Dallas, Amsterdam, Copenhagen, Helsinki, Leningrad, Stockholm and Bergen.

There were wonderful, fun, educational experiences for all of us. My wife and I are deeply grateful for the opportunities we had.

People say to me, "How fortunate those grandchildren are." I say, "How fortunate we grandparents are." We see our grandchildren every week anyway, but boat rides,

Disney World's many attractions, how far out in the ocean to ride waves, long plane rides to Amsterdam or from Mexico City to New York City and the like, lead to hundreds of recurring decisions, conflicts, fun times, pushing each other over in bed at times, and some growing experiences for all four of us.

Much of the time we catered to the wishes and tastes of our grandchildren, of course. It was primarily our gift of an interesting and educational vacation for them, but we will not forget the joys as well as the stresses of these wonderful times together!

The important point is: Who called the shots? Who had the final say? My wife and I did not always agree, of course, as with any two fairly intelligent people. Sometimes we took a vote on what to do. Two and two, however, didn't always make democracy easy. But the final arbiter if a procedural issue was involved, in anything that might affect the mental or physical well-being of the children, was the parents.

Before we bought tickets for a bull fight in Mexico City, we said to the parents, "Do you want them to see a bull fight at this stage of their lives?" We said to the parents, "Shall we decide whether a roller coaster is too dangerous for them or not?" From Dallas four years ago, we called the parents in Omaha and said, "*Jaws II* is on at a movie close to our hotel here; shall we take them?" (We had joked about some movies needing GPG—grandparental guidance—instead of PG rating). We saw *Jaws II* and with no bad effects on anyone.

Such matters as how many cokes a day were allowed, whether taking baths (for our grandson especially) and brushing teeth was to be monitored by us, how often sweets like candy bars between meals were to be allowed, when to go to bed at night, how much TV was to be allowed, and the like was checked with parents. Basically the letter of the law was followed.

After all, the parents didn't have a lot of extreme or absurd rules. They were willing to bend the schedules or the eating customs when reason called for it. But even if we had not agreed with their rules, their rules would have been enforced. Children need consistency, all authorities agree. This means that grandparents should aim at being consistent with parents if possible.

"Go ahead and eat this chocolate bar but don't tell your parents" or "Don't tell your daddy that I gave you this money" or "When you are at our house you can suspend the rules"—such remarks and the attitudes they reflect are not for the good of the children nor the good of interpersonal relations in the extended family.

The primary rule is: "Those who bring children into the world are the ones to bring up children in the world." The second is like unto it: "If you have any questions about what a child (grandchild in this case) should do, ask his parents."

P.S. *I've just shown our daughter a cartoon clipped from the* Saturday Review, *in which a middle age couple is sitting at cocktails with a younger couple (one of them apparently their child). The father announces, "We've decided not to have grandchildren."*

Grandparents Have Rights Too

THERE ARE TWO BIG problems that complicate the relationships of grown children and their parents. One, the children continue to feel that they have a divine right to call upon their parents at any time, like they did when they were young and small, and parents must respond. The other is the fact that so many people, as they get older, do not keep on growing and developing their own individual lives. They become parasites and passive, dependent persons, instead of courageous, creative, adventurous souls willing to risk change and suffer uncertainty.

I will devote the first half of this chapter to exploding the divine right theory of offspring; the second to exposing the passivity pattern of becoming helpless in the middle and latter periods of life.

The first is illustrated by the story of a little boy who was spending his vacation with his banker grandfather.

The sixty-year-old grandfather came home from a stressful day at his bank, slipped off his shoes, settled in his easy chair, and was spending a few minutes coaxing and, like Walt Whitman, inviting his soul. The grandson, six years old, burst into the room with, "Gramp, I want to ride the horses."

At that moment the grandfather had almost as soon have heard a fire alarm.

"No, Willie, Gramp has to rest a few minutes from a hard day at the office. Later."

"Okay," was William's slow and reluctant reply.

Five minutes later he was back with, "Okay, Gramp, it's time to ride the horses."

"No, William, I'm still tired and it takes longer than that to rest."

Five minutes later little Willie's patience ran out. The sun was getting lower by the minute, he noticed. This time it was, "Gramp, you've rested long enough now. It's time to ride the horses. It'll be getting dark before you know it."

"William Waters, I said I needed some rest, and you don't seem to understand that that takes time. Now go on out and play with Ole Cap (the dog) for a few minutes." This was more than Willie's frustration threshold was prepared for, so he made his best and final maneuver.

"Gramp, you don't seem to understand that grandfathers are supposed to do what their little grandsons ask them to."

That did it. The grandfather laughed, but he went out to bridle and saddle the horse.

"The Divine Right" Habit Peaks in Adolescence

The bad habits of allowing children to dominate are fostered especially during the teen years. Of course, the stage for adolescent problems, actually, is set in the early years—all the way from infancy on. Adults (parents) impose on each other or make demands or manipulate each other in front of the children. But even if they did not have too many faulty patterns in their family flow of circumstances, the pressures and needs of teenagers are so great that they easily fall into the habit of making exorbitant demands.

The movement to get free of childhood ways of relating to parents is not easy. It is characterized by puzzlement, irrationalities, feelings of not being loved on the part of children and of not being appreciated on the part of parents.

After all, how do you tell a child during the teen years that the house, including the furniture in his bedroom, is your property? That the car and the family income, including inheritance from your parents, is really yours? It makes him look like a free boarder or even an imposition on you, especially when the family budget is tight and the children's needs are escalating.

One parent had to say to an adolescent girl, "Look, I pay the phone bill around here. The telephone is mine. The house is mine. The land on which it is built is mine. I even bought the clothes on your back." At which the sixteen-year-old girl burst into tears and, before she migrated to her room, shouted: "Okay, I don't have any rights around here. Even the clothes on my back are not mine, you say. I'll leave. I don't belong here. I hear you. That is what you are trying to tell me. You don't want me. I get it."

She didn't leave. The father did not mean exactly what he said, but the thirty-dollar, long-distance charge on the phone bill had set him off. The situation was ambiguous. Situations are often confusing, to state it mildly, in families. That's why living together under one roof, especially during those growing-up years, is such a challenge to all concerned.

Somewhere between early adolescence and the early middle years, children have to learn that their parents have their own lives to lead, have rights of their own, and are not necessarily destined and foreordained to be forever devoted to their children's happiness.

LEVELING WITH EACH OTHER ABOUT RESTRUCTURING

The secret it seems is clear communication. It is especially important for parents and their adult children to level with each other on how they feel about the way they wish to relate to each other.

The severest attitude taken by parents in restructuring the relationship with their children is reflected in statements like: "You're on your own the minute you get married; from then on, don't expect anything from us." Or "Now that you are legal age, eighteen, stand on your own feet financially and otherwise; we have done our part by you." These harsh, cold sentences are rarely used, however. Most parents can't be this succinct or this stern (I almost said "realistic") in their shifting of gears in the child-launching period.

A more conciliatory viewpoint on the part of parents is, "We are going to stay out of your affairs now that you are married; but if you need us, call on us." What this means to the offspring may range anywhere from the children's never sharing any information about needs (financial, for example) to that of becoming adult parasites on their parents.

To repeat, the trick is in *leveling* with one another—checking out the situation.

Checking out means that one generation asks the other, "Do you wish to do so-and-so?" Or "How do you feel about this-or-that?" In such cases there should always be a clear understanding that the other is completely free to say, "Yes," or "No." There must never be an offer that cannot be turned down. Nor a hidden agenda that means, "If you don't agree to what I am proposing I'm gonna' be mad and will never again make a similar offer to you."

There is not just one way to relate to your children. Some parents, particularly those who have several children, become super-cautious not to do for one child more than for another, lest there be hard feelings and jealousy. Others draw the line on helping when the children marry or when they leave home. Some will help their offspring until they get on their feet financially. A larger number stand by to help in time of sickness, business failure, need for continued education, or divorce crises, or even to help with the education of grandchildren.

One parent, when asked how he handled the matter of giving out money to his child said: "I waited until he learned to stand on his own feet, make his own decisions, and not make demands; then I began to lavish him with things. If he demanded things, I would not give him the time of day. I feel very strongly that people should not invade one another's privacy or make demands on one another, even if they are related by blood or marriage. Invading or demanding leads to resentment and conflict and injury. Now when children get completely over the idea that their parents are an unlimited source from which they can draw time or money anytime they wish, it becomes a whole different ball game. Then you can make offers, add to their estate, put yourself out for them or be as generous as you enjoy being, as long as you both agree that you feel right about it."

In one counseling situation where ill will had developed between parents and children, I said to the mother (the dominant one of the two parents), "Why did you lend this money when you were not able to and, as you say, when they are living in luxury beyond yours?" She said, "I thought they needed it, but I thought they would at least be grateful." The father said, "She was always too soft with the kids and could never say no."

I picked up on the word *grateful*. I explained that gratitude is usually the last emotion we develop on the road to maturity. Some people never grow up enough to be grateful. Most children are not grateful to their parents until they are in their mid-twenties. Besides, exchanging things or favors for love or gratitude is not a procedure that works out very well.

Then we got down to the business of leveling with the children about the fact that they (the parents) felt the need to live and enjoy some of the fruit of their labors, and that they would be relating to their children on a more adult-adult basis from now on. The husband was convinced that I was right on the beam. It was not hard to see that the oversacrificial mother was afraid to give up her sacrificial pattern. No doubt sacrificing gave her life meaning.

I have to admit, however, that leveling does not always work. Some parents just do not learn, either from books, counselors, or experience.

The worse case I ever had experience with came to my attention when I was on a talk show called "Nightbeat" in Kansas City.

A young woman with a baby nine months old and a hard-working husband called in with a "What in the world am I going to do with my mother-in-law who is ruining my marriage and my baby?" question.

The situation was this. Both of the parents worked. In spite of their protests, his mother, who lived a few blocks away was causing them trouble continuously. Fairly well off, she had never worked out of the home, and she had lost her husband in an automobile accident two years before. The couple "had to get married," to the horror of the mother and other conservative relatives, but they loved each other and were making it pretty well, except—here was the rub.

Since he was an only child and since the mother had a fairly fat purse and a big heart, she insisted that they rent an apartment a few blocks from her home for which she bought most of the furniture. They appreciated this. The trouble, however, began when she insisted on making them her whole life. She told them what groceries to buy, how to raise their baby, who to have in as friends, where to go to church, nothing was omitted. She even came over to their apartment regularly and rearranged the furniture and threw away some of their clothes that she didn't like. There was always something she changed, in spite of their protests. The climax came when she, without consulting them, called in decorators and did over two rooms, changing to colors the daughter-in-law hated, and without even warning them what she was up to. That was the limit.

The show host and I asked the usual questions about what they had tried. Yes, they had told her how angry they were. Yes, they were perfectly able to finance themselves and their child—she was a competent waitress and he, a trained welder. Yes, they had been to a family counselor, with her, but it made no difference in her behavior. They had even changed the locks on the apartment doors, and she had called a locksmith on some pretense and had a key made for herself.

In desperation one of us, the host or I, the guest consultant, said, "Have you thought of moving out of town? Nothing else seems to work."

"Yes, her husband and she both would like to move to the West Coast; they liked Portland, Oregon, where some of her relatives lived." Our response was, "It seems that you have already tried everything we have suggested. Think about moving to the West Coast." We were almost facetious, barely serious at best.

You won't believe what happened. The caller's husband was driving home from work, listening to "Nightbeat." When he got home, they had a brief conversation, a fast packing of their suitcases, and away they went to Portland, Oregon, in the middle of the night. We know because the program had an agreement with callers that long-distance, collect calls would be accepted. A few nights later, the couple called from Oregon and reported how good they felt about their decision. If that mother had been listening to "Nightbeat" regularly, I would probably have not lived to tell this true story.

This case is extreme, I grant, but only the Lord knows how many couples have accepted transfers, or even requested them, to get away from dominating in-laws. And I have known grandparents who retired to warmer climates as they got older because the climate they really were escaping was the hate and misunderstanding and ill will of one or more children.

But in spite of the failure of leveling in the case just given, it usually works for people who try to behave rationally. So let us look more closely at some of our parental motivations and why our courage fails us when we try to be authentic individuals as well as unselfish givers. No doubt, our behavior is related to self images and meaning.

DON'T TRY TO MAKE UP FOR THE PAST

Finding meaning in giving to children and grandchildren is one thing. But another more common motivation, in my counseling experience, is parents who are trying to make up for their past failures in parenting. Given: a child who feels that he has a divine right to drain the parents' till, and a parent who has a deep need (real or imagined) to atone for the past failures. With this situation you have a perfect setting for conflict, confusion, and destructive confrontation.

It would seem to be a workable arrangement: A masochist (one who hurts himself or herself) and a sadist (one who hurts another). However, it doesn't work that well usually. The reason, probably, lies in the difference between conscious and non-conscious reasons for particular behaviors.

It reminds us of the masochist who said to the sadist: "Hurt me." The sadist refused.

For instance, the Wilsons reared two children, a son and a daughter. The son is now married and has two children. The daughter has her own career but is extravagant, self-centered, demanding, and basically a *taking* person.

Mr. and Mrs. Wilson both worked hard in middle class jobs. Mr. Wilson traveled, so felt that he never spent as much time with his children as they deserved. Both Mr. and Mrs. Wilson are devoted to the grandchildren, but their daughter sees to it that she is given something every time her brother's children receive something.

After seeking counseling, Mr. and Mrs. Wilson faced the fact that their daughter, and to some extent their son, had learned to get things from them by inducing guilt.

The children had used all the tricks, embodied in such dialogue as, "Don't you love your grandchildren?"

"You gave to them (the son's children) so you have to be fair by giving as much to me."

"I don't want you to do this unless you feel like it, but I don't know how we will get by."

The parents' damaging self-talk slipped out occasionally in, "I don't want them to have to suffer the hardship that we went through."

"We want the best for our grandchildren."

"We can't afford to make Cynthia think we love them more than we do her."

"We never could do for them as they were growing up what some parents did for their children."

When the counselor said, "Is this what *you both* want

to do? Or are you trying to keep everybody in a good humor?" They both agreed that they were often doing things under the pressure of guilt and feelings of inadequacy as parents. They were acting under the duress of their children's expectations rather than their own generosity. They decided to make a stand. From now on they would not give in; instead, they would give when they chose to and when they considered it wise.

It took the children several months to believe that their parents were standing tall and refusing to be pressured. Nevertheless, they learned a valuable lesson—one should never pressure their parents into doing things for them. Request, maybe. Pressure, never. It is a lesson that may help the son and daughter-in-law when it's time for them to wean their own children from parental dependency.

LOOKING AT THE WHY OF GIVING

In addition to making up for past failures or relieving guilt feelings, there are other motives for giving unwisely to children and grandchildren. Of course, the question of what is wise will be largely a matter of opinion. But when parents indulge offspring to their own deprivation, or when their giving distorts reality for the children or grandchildren, when donations cause conflict between either set of spouses, or when later the parents regret that they sacrificed, it may be considered unwise.

The motive may be the desire to be super grandparents, a grandiose concept of what it means to be unselfish, or for that matter, "to be seen of men." But the reward is dubious. As a rule of thumb, we may assume that our giving of money, time, or other kinds of gifts, will be wise or unwise depending on what it does to persons. To test whether our giving is successful, we must ask ourselves whether it may in the long run bring satisfaction to everyone concerned. This cannot always be known ahead of time, but in many situations any person who will stop and think can see that giving will in the long run hurt rather than help.

It is easy for unthinking grandparents to take the irresponsible road of saying, "If I want to give money or time or gifts, who is to say that I shouldn't?" This sounds sensible at first, but in the long run it may work out badly. After all, who does not wish that their children, and grandchildren, will rise up and call them blessed (Prov. 31:28)? If our giving is stubborn aggression, it will simply engender resentment.

When we put out for our children or grandchildren, we should ask ourselves some pertinent questions.

Does this giving contribute to unrealistic expectations on the part of the receiver, children or grandchildren? Some parents set precedents by giving to their children when they first marry or when the grandchildren are born, then are surprised when the children expect them to continue at the same rate later. Some become rescuers in time of crisis, then wonder why their offspring have so many crises. Perhaps they came to assume that the great troubleshooters would continue to rise to the occasion.

Am I giving out of love, freely, and without feeling duress? Much giving of all kinds is not from love or the joy of giving, but because someone expects it or puts the bee on you. The kindest thing some parents do for their children is put them on their own and refuse to "pull their chestnuts out of the fire." This goes for grandchildren, too, at times.

Also, can I afford this time or money or inconvenience at this point in my life? I have seen parents who sacrificed for their children, only to have the children indulge themselves unnecessarily, and smile later at the stupidity of their parents. There is nothing wrong with putting yourself out for children or grandchildren, if they are actually in need and the giving says to them, "This is how much I love you" or "We are all in this together." But depleting one's self or depriving others in order to indulge children or grandchildren rarely helps anyone.

For example, a fifty-five-year-old woman, who lost her husband three years ago, insists on working, saving, and not really enjoying her own life. Her only child tells me that her mother has no life of her own. "She lives for me and my husband and our two children. I have told her over and over, 'Enjoy your own life. We don't need your money. Daddy left it to you. We would actually be happier if you would make yourself happier by traveling or whatever you want to do.' " Did she? No, she preferred to blame her stinginess on the depression years, and on the habits of hard work she and her late husband had developed, and on her religion which taught "deny yourself." What a pity! And what a burden to her daughter!

FIND SOMETHING IMPORTANT TO DO

We come now to the heart of the problem which is parasitic and masochistic experiences. In simple words, those who cling to their children or grandchildren and oversacrifice for them are doing so because they do not have a life of their own. They do not have anything important to do. They have ceased to be creative, if in fact they ever were.

Many grandparents will protest that there is nothing more important to them than their children and grandchildren.

"They are my whole life."

"You cannot imagine what these grandkids mean to me."

"I'd give my right arm for any one of them."

"What's more important to me than my own flesh and blood?"

These are sentences which one hears.

Sometimes I call this "grandparent insanity." The grandparent almost seems to go into a trance when one of the grandchildren walks into the room. Utter irrationality takes over. There is an extravagant exaggeration of the grand offspring's brains, looks, prowess, and attainments, often outright lying about attainments—much more than about their own children. Why wouldn't they put themselves out for these prodigies? Such people inhabit this planet only a few times within the century. The gods have descended. Let us bow down in reverence. Of course, I'm exaggerating, but such seems to be the story of grandparent insanity.

It is well known to psychologists and other social scientists, as well as to religious leaders, that people tend to worship others (put them on pedestals) in direct proportion to their own lack of self-esteem and to their self-denigration. In other words, you put others *up* as a result of your putting yourself *down*. Low rating of self leads to overrating of others.

So parents who found great importance in building careers, rearing and developing offspring, proving themselves in the community, and even making their mark in church, synagogue, or mosque, now are running out of tasks. They about have it made in their vocations (usually both husband and wife have). Their children have been launched and turned out pretty well. They may even move half around the world. In community, club, church, or lodge they have held most of the offices (if they are leaders), so there is nowhere else to go.

Add to this the fact that in a youth and beauty-oriented culture, and in a society that promotes and values production, the grand generation has to find new values. Even though we have more trouble hearing high pitched and low pitched sounds, have a slower reaction speed, and are less agile, our I.Q. shows little change, contrary to popular opinion. The real problems of middle-aged and older people seems to be that we over-react to our failures (like poor memory for recent events), narrow down our attention and emotional investments, throw ourselves out of gear, and spend too much time looking backward rather than forward.

In other words, when we have to turn loose of some things, like certain physical activities or a job or friendships, we postpone getting involved in new ones.

One of the most common complaints I hear from concerned, sincerely interested, and loving children is expressed in sentences such as the following: "What can we do to get our parents to live their own lives? We appreciate their eagerness to help us and to spend time with our children, but we worry about them. As they have gotten older, they have narrowed down their interest, shut out friends their own age, and denied themselves new interests and enjoyments. We hate to say it this way, but they are becoming a burden to us. We don't want to be their only friends. What can we do to stimulate them to keep growing on their own?"

Stimulating them seldom gets the job done. Motivation comes from within. Our culture tends to leave the impression with people that if they prepare well and work hard in their youth, by middle age or a little later they will have it made. Some do economically. Some do so far as fame or reputation is concerned.

The truth seems to be that we never get it made, as persons. Each period of life has its distinctive temptations and needs new challenges. Meaning is found not in status, nor in attainment. The process of being creators, since we are made in the image of the Creator, becomes our primary task as long as we live. When we cease to create and become hangers-on to our children or grandchildren, we may easily become depressed or hurt or resentful or just bored. Creativity is often the alternative to one of these emotional states.

Nothing, then, must prevent grandparents from growing. Not the pressure of family custom, the duress of crisis needs of children or grandchildren, nor their own habit of "putting the children first."

And do not expect people around you to give you permission to live. The emancipation proclamation must come from within each grandparent. It may be that freedom will consist of investing your lives deeply, fully, and sacrifically, in your children and grandchildren. In some cases that becomes the climax of great living. However, it must be from choice, not from pressure.

Free to live as we decide, under God, and for whatever we see is important. This is the right of every human being, and especially grandparents.

Seeing Your Children
as Colleagues

IN 1976 JAMES A. LEVINE, a professor at Wellesley College, published a rather perceptive book entitled *Who Will Raise the Children?* It was a good study of the changing role of the father in the home but overlooked completely the part grandparents are playing. One thing became clear, however, somebody has to do the parenting, and it is an enticing and fascinating job, as some househusbands even are finding out.

In 1977, Margaret Mead, the noted anthropologist, wrote an article in March issue of *The Saturday Evening Post* entitled "Grandparents as Educators." By education she included speech, manners, morals, skills, restraining our impulses, postponing gratification, participating in social life, and the whole process of enculturation, as she calls it. This would include religion, recreation, and value systems. At one point she says, "Somehow we have to get the older people, grandparents, widows and widowers, spinsters and bachelors, back close to children if we are to restore a sense of community, a knowledge of the past and a sense of the future to today's children" (p. 58). It is a part of her solution to the very rapid change that has taken place in our society. I agree. All of us feel the strain and confusion of the accelerated change that is all about us. We may well find the crux of the solution right in the family, especially in the intergenerational interactions of the family. Let's hope so.

This will not happen, however, unless both sides of the intergenerational fence understand the rules of the game, at least the principles of keeping good relationships.

As I pointed out in chapter 1, parents are the real authority in the lives of children, and no one is to manipulate anyone, neither parents nor grandparents, and certainly not children. Now I would like to deal with some positive ways that grandparents can assist and collaborate with parents in this delightful but complicated task of rearing children. It will require maturity, generosity, and some self-sacrifice, but this collaboration can be fun and an adventure if both sides are careful to be creative and constructive. Barring some real emotional or character quirks, three or four adults, depending on whether both grandparents are living, should be able to get along. And if there are such quirks, they should be evaluated and, if possible, overcome, so that there can be the flow of honest communication and consequently a working approach to doing what is best for the grandchildren.

The secret is to see each other as colleagues or collaborators, not competitors nor conquerors. The two parents are the last word on the subject when decisions about the children have to be made. But so often one set of grandparents gets at odds with one or both of the parents (or even at odds with the other set of grandparents), and we have a "win or bust" pattern of behavior. As usual, who loses in win-lose games? You win the game or argument, but you lose the relationship. Everybody loses, but especially the children. They deserve better than this; but often adults act like children, locking horns over some issue that is usually not important enough to fight about. Or they get into a death struggle to prove one right and the other wrong and come out back to back.

Everyone, in such a power struggle, will allege loudly that they love the children. Each may be saying that they are trying to save the children from the harmful effect the other is having on the "sweet young things." I have seen parents vow that the grandparents were damaging the children, over such minor things as the grandparents letting the children sit up too late at night. Others complain that the grandparents are damaging the children by being too strict. The fact is, children do need consistency, but they are not so frail that they are ruined or traumatized by some inconsistencies between parents or between parents and grandparents. Human beings just aren't that fragile.

COLLEAGUES IN CREATING ECOLOGY

What does matter is the atmosphere of the surroundings in which we grow up. *Ecology* is the popular and modern word for the intangible but tremendously important facet of interaction, of being together, which we call climate or atmosphere. It is the vapor-like sphere of relationships that surround our lives. Words like cold, hot, stern, comfortable, painful, suffocating, dangerous, healthy, contaminated, happy, loving, distant describe how we experience relationships, how we sense or feel the interaction with people, pets, living creatures all around us.

It does not take a research scientist to know that children are very much aware and tremendously affected by the psychic or spiritual climate around us. They sense it long before they could put it accurately into words. Metaphors abound:

"Our home was like a jail."

"It was the worse mess of a home (she was not speaking of sanitation) I ever saw; and I had a ringside seat."

"Everything was cold and stiff in our home, like we were hollow and plastic, no heart."

I have heard these remarks over and over.

But as I have been saying, grandparenting and the joys of it, or the advantages of it, are not always an unmixed blessing. Three of my friends each report very different experiences.

One says, "I did everything I could to avoid the only grandfather I knew. He was a regular old fuss-budget, stern, critical, afraid we would break or misplace something. He was a religious fanatic, and everytime I got around him he started preaching about how rotten the world was and how people didn't have any respect for each other. I think of him as a perfect example of Mark Twain's expression 'He was a good man in the worst sense of the word.'"

The other says, "When I get old I want to be the kind of man my grandfather was. He and his wife lived together for sixty-two years, and they always seemed to have something going between them. We used to go out, one child at a time to visit them—I don't know whose idea that was, maybe theirs, for they had good common sense, and they never let us get by with way-out things. But they took time with us, played with us, took us with them on chores and errands, asked our opinions when they had decisions to make. They always made us feel important. I really guess it was my grandfather's example that made me decide to be a Christian when I did. I knew that he had something, and my grandmother, too.

Another friend says, "I just can't wait to be a grandfather." His wife is not quite so hot on the subject. "I'm going to do for my grandkids what I was too busy to do for my children as they were growing up and I was getting started in my career. I'm going to take them places and give them things and let them do some things I was too hard-nosed to let my children do. I guess I wanted mine to be perfect."

My response to another friend, about these remarks, was: "Sounds to me like he is on a guilt trip, trying to atone for his failures with his own children. The Lord have mercy on his grandchildren if their parents don't fend him off when he gets overzealous. If they don't, society may have to teach these kids that the world is not made up of grandparents like him, and God is not Santa Claus."

It was emotional ecology that the Bible dealt with, frankly and recurrently, in both Testaments. Joseph's brothers "hated him, and could not speak peaceably to him" (Gen. 37:4). "Like as a father pitieth his children, so the Lord pitieth them that fear him. For he knoweth our frame; he remembereth that we are dust" (Ps. 103:13, kjv). "Have done with spite and passion, all angry shouting and cursing, and bad feelings of every kind. Be generous to one another, tender-hearted, forgiving one another as God in Christ forgave you" (Eph. 4:31–32, neb).

In this last quotation, the Christian atmosphere is being described. If we can keep the ecology clear of dominance, hate, revenge and verbal acting out, the channels of communication can be kept open, hope will spring eternal in the human breast, and the extended family (relatives) can grow together and share each other's joys and sorrows.

The problems and the stress situations which arise in the interaction in families cannot be eliminated by ten easy rules—rules that try to fit all family patterns into one mold—and certainly not by freezing the family customs and turning the clock back to another generation's way of life. It will take love, patience, talking our way into a meeting of the minds, and especially maturity.

HELP IN TIMES OF CRISIS

Families still stand by, support, comfort, and encourage each other in times of stress—illness, loss of job, legal trouble, and especially and most frequently divorce. However, being helpful in time of crisis works both ways, parents to children and children to parents. Whoever is most mobile and accessible tends to respond to the need. Generally single persons are more mobile than married. But among the elderly, couples are more mobile than singles. Mobility is based on rising to the occasion in time of crisis or moving from one geographical area to another.

Usually the crises which evoke heroic and unselfish action are on a short term basis. They involve being there after a baby is born, especially on the part of the girl's mother. Or doing chores. Or taking parents for chemotherapy or dentist appointments. Or where both children work, a grandparent may stay with a sick child who is too sick to go to school.

I have referred to the divorce crisis. It is of tremendous help emotionally if a person who faces the inevitable divorce can tell his parents and/or grandparents and not be judged. I am seeing more and more women—usually the hardest hit financially in a divorce proceeding—whose parents or grandparents can say: "We will stand by you; do what is best for you and the children. You are not a loser just because the marriage failed." Such support by the man's older relatives is equally encouraging.

All pastoral counselors, social workers, psychologists, and psychiatrists who counsel many families can cite some horrible examples of how the extended family often lets the divorcing person down. These range from upbraidings, to misjudging motives, to not speaking to each other, to complete boycotting at family get-togethers, to homicides. Extreme cases are rare, of course, but when we develop more facilities for studying the qualities of interpersonal relationships beyond the nuclear family, I judge that we will find it not uncommon that most families go through periods of estrangement and downright hate. Instead, superficial (duty oriented) ways of relating are more common than genuine fondness, enjoyment of each other, and sincere love.

LEISURE TIME: A NEW PROBLEM

Families must also face a comparatively new problem. I speak of the family relations of those over forty-five. I say forty-five because grandparenting usually begins in the late forties, especially for those who had their children a little late. At this time in their lives, and progressively as they grow older, grandparents begin to have more leisure time—time to be with their grandchildren if they wish to, and if they know how.

But many grandparents today did not have much grandparenting themselves. They either did not have grandparents living close to them or if they did their grandparents had no leisure time. At the turn of the century two-thirds of the U.S. male population over sixty-five were members of the labor force. But in 1975 only one-third were holding jobs. Add to this the number of women who work outside the home, and we see a rather varied social situation. There's more leisure, but also there are many grandparents as well as parents working forty or more hours a week. It makes one wonder "Who will raise the kids?" Somebody has to parent.

However, in spite of mobility (one family out of five moving their residence every year), grandparents and their children do see each other often. Studies show that three-fourths of older people in the U.S. have living grandchildren. About the same proportion see their grandchildren every week or so. Eighty percent of those who have ever married have living children. And about the same percent of those (sixty-five or over) live less than an hour away from one of their children. (Parents tend to migrate to be near one of their children when they retire, but few wish to live in the same domicile with a child—the exceptions being when a child is still unmarried, and then as they get older, women more often than men live with a single daughter.)

Furthermore, one study (Reubin Hill, et al., in Minneapolis) showed that grandchildren visit their grandparents at least once a month. Another (Harris and Associates in North Carolina) showed that 55 percent of parents have seen their children in the last day or so and 81 percent within the last week or so. This would certainly indicate the accessibility of grandchildren.

How little we have tapped this incredible resource!

Education: A Family Affair

Grandparents are sometimes used as school "teacher's aids" in some sections of the country. And foster grandparenting programs are being developed in some communities for children who do not have grandparents available. What a blessing to the grandparents! It may offer them a program for feeling needed and useful. And what a help to children, especially when these grandparents relate to them in imaginative and healthy ways. For children, this foster grandparent is someone who can spend time with them and teach them some of the needed skills that working parents may not have the time or patience to do.

Much teaching is incidental and occasional (arising when the occasion calls for it). Some learning fails because there is no felt need when the adults (like teachers) have it scheduled. But a willing grandparent may teach a child anything from how to tie a knot to how to bake a cake. The incidental part may involve not only facts or skills, but such elements as learning patience, how to finish one job before you start another, how to be close to another human being and enjoy frankness and honesty about our own limitations. Children are impressionable, especially when you are not trying to impress them.

I hear parents complain sincerely and fervently about how much of their time is spent in chauffeuring and helping children practice whatever they are trying to learn. In the summertime when school is out or when the home is a one-parent home, by death or divorce, important learning may be in order. What an opportunity for grandparents! As the child gets older you may have to take along the child's or young person's friend, but that too may be a good learning experience for all. We have relegated thousands of children to camps and paid adults, usually young adults, to direct them. I'm not disparaging such camps. In fact I see them as badly needed. But camps will not take the place of grandparents or foster grandparents who will take time to share themselves and their skills, and even learn new skills in order to invest more intelligently in the citizens of tomorrow.

I cannot emphasize too strongly that the important learning in life, so far as everyday living and effective coping with life is concerned, is not something you learn from a manual or a how-to-book.

In our society we tend to turn much of what is important in life over to some institution such as the school or the church, expecting it to teach the necessary information or skills. But grandparents often have a unique opportunity to do some effective teaching. When the situation calls for learning there may even be a request like, "Grandpa, will you show me how to. . . ?" Such learning grows out of a healthy, expanding, creative mind reaching out to know what the world is like or learning coping skills. There seems to be more openness then. The grandparent who is alert to these occasions may become a good teacher. The material may range from how to repair an electric cord to how to look up a verse in a Bible concordance. The important factors are alertness to the child's openness-to-learning and patience in practicing good learning procedures.

Caring parents, even stepparents, will be delighted when children learn certain things from their grandparents. When a parent comes out with an exclamation of surprise, "Where in the world did you learn that?" and the child says "At Granny's house last summer" there will usually be feelings of gratitude. After all, most modern parents are so busy, especially in the dual career family, that they know they do not have the time that is needed to teach their children all the incidental skills that may add to the repertoire for the competency of their offspring. In our culture we are about to admit that the job the home did in the first half of the century, of turning our children over to the schools with an unspoken mandate "Educate them for life; that's what we are paying you for" was a cop out. Or over to the church with a "Teach them religion; you claim that's what you want to do." Education is a family affair and grandparents are an important part of the act.

Give the Parents a Vacation

And speaking of harried parents who are busy and who need a vacation from their children, grandparents have a place to fill here.

Surveys show that an alarmingly high percentage of parents say that if they had it to do over, they would not have children. (It doesn't matter whether it is 40 or 70 percent; it is significant.) But we need to ask ourselves why this discontent with the parenting function? It has been known for at least twenty-five years that having children puts a marriage under stress. Yes, there are rewards to child rearing. There are meaningful satisfactions and challenges. But most of us grandparents have forgotten the stresses and strains, the worries and the weariness, even the anxiety and the anguish that come with child rearing.

When we were in the child rearing stage of our lives, we joked about how children get under your feet when they are little and walk on your heart when they are teenagers. Some of us even admitted that children are doubtful blessings from the Lord. The Psalmist said, "Children are a blessing from the Lord, blessed is the man who has his quiver full." That was in the bow and arrow age when agricultural advantages in having boys especially was great. They needed men fighters to defend themselves from neighboring tribes, too. And they had relatives around them to help rear them. This is still true in many countries, e.g., China. But, now, with both parents leaving the domicile most days, and both grandparents often working too, even if the parents understand the importance of "quality time," they feel guilty when they see their children clamoring for more time. After twenty-five years of the pill and similar contraceptive devices, it is no wonder that some married people choose to have few or no children. And when they have one or two, they begin to quiver, especially the women, when they hear the Psalmist or anyone else talk about having a quiver full.

There is much less quivering, especially with rage, when there are relief patterns woven into the cloth of the weekly living of parents. "I love my children," one mother told me, "but it is the sameness and the constancy, the day-by-dayness of it that gets me down. If only Tom and I could get a weekend to ourselves occasionally, or a night out every week or so, but we can't afford to hire someone to stay with the children." Many parents are not so frank, but they are equally frustrated and may be angry deep down. And the children suffer.

With this couple, and many others, the real need is for trustworthy temporary parent surrogates who will take over the children, and sometimes the house, and say to the couple or the single parent, "We will take care of the children. Just tell them to accept our authority, and we will accept your rules. When you get back, the chances are all will be well. You can have a mini-vacation from parenting. In the meantime, we will have a good time filling in."

Who Is Selfish?

It is easy for older people to see the younger generation as selfish and materialistic and unwilling to put themselves out for their children. We have just gone through a "me-decade" and there is a kind of narcissistic cult that is gaining ground in our culture. Altruism has never been easy for human beings. The flesh and the spirit, to use Paul's language, are always striving with each other. I do not think, however, that parents today are any more self-centered or frustrated or full of stress, than I or my parents were. They simply have a different set of stressors and some new problems, especially agenda anxiety. There simply is not time enough, in spite of all that we hear about leisure, to do all that we would like to do with our children that they could use profitably.

This is especially true of the single parent—the parent whose child was born when there has been no marriage or the parent who has lost a mate by death, or (the larger number) the parent who has been divorced and has the custody of the children. One set of grandparents, and sometimes both sets, may be extremely valuable here. This goes for other close relatives too, unmarried aunts or uncles, married aunts or uncles, and sometimes great-grandparents. We have talked so much in the last few years about the nuclear family that we have forgotten the importance of the extended family. Rearing children is, ideally, a joint venture. We need all hands on deck.

So who is selfish? Of course, there is a wise selfishness on the part of any of us. As we will discuss in a later chapter, none of us should allow our children or our grandchildren to impose on us. However, I think selfishness of the crippling sort is seen most blatantly in the grandparent who says, "I raised my own kids and it was not easy. Let young people today raise their kids. It won't hurt them to sacrifice a little." I am reminded of Jesus' words about saving your life by losing it (Matt. 10:39). It seems to be a spiritual, and I dare say eternal, law that if you look out for Number One only, you will soon be by yourself and wondering where everyone else went. What you sow you reap.

After all is said and done about "oughts" and "shoulds" (ethics and morals), life is based primarily on reciprocity. It is the major ingredient in almost everything—our friendships, our religion, and our family life. Lovers give and take to meet each other's needs. Religion is based on such ideas as "Freely you have received, freely give" (Matt. 10:8), and there are numerous passages of Scripture that say forgive as you have been forgiven.

The absorbers, the sponges, and the me-firsters, cannot (or will not) practice the Golden Rule, regardless of how it shines or how often it is repeated. In order to live by the Golden Rule we have to learn to feel for people, to sense what others' needs are, and care enough about them to aim some of our behavior at meeting their needs. It requires awareness and a willingness to put ourselves out for each other.

For example, one set of parents I know gives special privileges to their children in proportion to their children's willingness to spend some time each month with two great-grandmothers who are in nearby nursing homes. The dialogue at one point between the parents and two children went like this:

"We are all aware that Memaw and Geegee (the names

they had attached to their great-grandmothers) would rather see you kids than to see us. I guess you must have something that we do not. And we realize that you would rather be with your friends." This is the father talking. He has very fine sensibilities concerning interpersonal relations. "But we do not intend for you to enjoy privileges without responsibilities."

The eleven-year-old, youngest child, piped up. "What do you mean? We are responsible, aren't we? What does that have to do with visiting Geegee?" ("Geegee" stood for great-grandmother).

The father: "I'll tell you what it has to do with it. A lot of what your mother and I are, is due to these once marvelous people. I know they are not interesting for you to be with, especially like your friends are, but they don't see many people other than those people in the rest home, their own age. They watch TV and keep up with the world, but you know what they say they enjoy most with their narrowed-down schedule. You kids. You are the only great-grandchildren close by."

"Yeah, Memaw looks forward to your visit more than she does mine, she even tells me. It hurts my feelings," the mother said half facetiously.

"The principle is simply this," continued the father, who was really the moral leader in the family, and sometimes over-moralized, "a great deal of life is giving to those who have given to you and not being self-centered. I don't think I'm saying this right, but we owe a lot to those who have invested in our lives when we needed them most. We are going to be old sometime and so are you. It is not just having anybody to visit you when you are in a retirement home that matters, but you want to see people who are your own flesh and blood, who are yours."

"But we can't find much to talk about. Our interests are different," the other child, a thirteen-year-old girl, responded.

"Maybe that's the point," mother said, "they don't have many interests. Their world is narrow. But you tell me you always find things to talk about. It may be that just being there, taking the time and going to the trouble of visiting them is what does them so much good."

Then the father concluded, "I hate to have to pressure you into doing this, but those who plan to visit them and who find a time and put it in their agenda will be rewarded by some special privileges. I don't know what they will be. It will not be a trip around the world. But you know that you are always asking to go somewhere or get something. I just want you to know that opportunities and privileges you are given will follow what you have done for someone else, like your grandmothers. I'm not trying to be hard nosed about it, but that is the way life is. You give before you get."

Whether this father's thesis is perfect or not, it is clear that he was trying to instill in his children the idea that you can't be a me-first-last-and-always person and come out ahead morally.

If grandparents did not serve any other purpose to their grandchildren, they certainly are for them an occasion for loving and the objects for loving deeds. If we have reared our children to be thoughtful, compassionate people, they will likely direct their children in being thoughtful and helpful to us. If we haven't and if they do not teach their children to be respectful and helpful to "their elders," it is very unlikely that they will get respect from their heirs fifty years from now. Maybe this is one of God's eternal laws, as I have suggested.

Only last week a seventy-five-year-old client of mine told me how this is working in his family.

He lives in a small house next door to the sixth of his seven children. His wife died seven months ago and he is dealing with the residue of his grief and some depression. All of his children live within a hundred miles of him.

Having suffered a severe stroke in January, he gets around with his cane, cares for his dog, watches his two grandchildren next door, cooks most of his meals, listens to his music, and copes with life pretty well.

Recently his daughter and son-in-law, next door, sent a note suggesting that each of the children come and get their father one day a month and keep him twenty-four hours, if convenient, to alleviate his loneliness. He reported that some of his children were angry at the suggestion. He understood how busy they were, he said.

Then, he began to recount how some of his small grandchildren would climb up in his lap and smile at him and ask him questions, and even request to come out and spend the day with him. He enjoys playing checkers with them. He cried as he told me. I could see how much it meant to him. I could imagine how much it meant to his grandchildren.

That Talking Money

This leads to one of the trickiest problems that relatives face, or families in general for that matter. Money.

Thomas Fuller, a seventeenth century writer, said it succinctly: "Money talks." It announces our sins and heralds our good qualities. The Apostle Paul spoke of the love of money as the root of all evils (1 Tim. 6:10). And Jesus drove the greedy money changers out of the temple (John 2:13–17). We joke about the importance or unimportance of money, swear to high heaven that we cannot take it with us when we die, but do all we can to amass as much of it as possible, all the time vowing that we do not care one thing about it, only what it will buy. Well, la-de-dah, that's what money is for, no one loves money for how big a wall it will paper, except possibly a few quirked people.

Money is what families fight about and get estranged

over, even get to where they will not speak to each other.

In the in-law constellation it becomes especially precarious. I told my son-in-law shortly after he married our only child, "We may have some money that we will want to share with you and Pat (our daughter), but I have seen so many families that have misunderstood each other over money that I approach the subject with fear and trembling. If it ever becomes a threat to your manhood or your sense of family autonomy, tell us. You won't have to tell us but once. We grew up during the Depression, and we would like to keep your family from going through the deprivation that we faced. There will be no strings attached to what we give. We do not ask for gratitude, nor will we try to tell you how to spend money. The truth is, we give selfishly, for the sheer joy of sharing our blessings."

That was quite a speech, wasn't it? But we have tried to live up to it. At least, so far there has been no confusion, partly because he was sure enough of his manhood and their integrity, and our integrity, that he could allow us this satisfaction.

It must be admitted, however, that the problems are different when there are several children and more grandchildren. Even if one child is in dire need, the parent has to ask himself/herself how the others may feel about a loan or a gift to this one child. Sibling rivalry is usually present in the family. If a loan is made, is there a note given? And will it ever be paid back so that it may get into the estate for inheritance purposes?

It is not uncommon for parents to make loans or gifts to children, or even to grandchildren, to great advantage when a crisis occurs, or when a home or condominium is to be purchased. This may be a welcomed opportunity for the grandparent. I recommend it, if proper reality factors are taken into consideration. I do not recommend that money be given or loaned to one of the couple, the blood child, and not to the other, the in-law. "Whom God hath joined together, let not man put asunder." Money relayed to one may be planting the seeds that will wedge the couple apart.

In spite of many possible hazards, however, I have seen more blessings than handicaps come from assisting young families in the early years. Otherwise, they often inherit the same money at a time in their lives when it is not especially needed and after Uncle Sam has pinched a hunk off the top. In such cases, where the money is not particularly needed, I have seen only a few rare souls who leave their money to good causes that will make the world a better place in which to live. Maybe the reluctance to do this grows out of a fear that the children will be offended.

But the money problem comes up in a thousand little ways. Grandchildren may try to wangle money or gifts out of grandparents when the parents have already said that the child could not have the toy or the pony or the car, or whatever.

Or to mention another problem, both parents and children may connive to get "dear old soft grandpa or grandmother" to come across with a gift or loan in order to save their own money for some other expenditure. A rule of thumb would seem to be: Never fall for deception or pressure; if they can't be honest and open, have no part in the transaction.

Money like every other aspect of intergenerational transactions will depend on the rules of the game. Maybe the following guidelines will be starters on the road to good human relations, whether about money, vacations, babysitting, or sudden crises in the family:

1. Don't try to control the agenda—how much time you spend with children or grandchildren.

2. Never say things about children or grandchildren behind their backs. You will likely be quoted and, as likely as not, misquoted.

3. Don't specialize in being brutally frank. That's for brutes.

4. When disagreements occur, admit that you may be (or have been, as the case may be) wrong.

5. Find ways to honestly say something good to your children and grandchildren. Enough people will criticize or tear them down. They need strokes and warm fuzzies—gestures that produce feelings of approval and regard.

6. Don't be afraid to trust your own insights or hunches. They may be the leadership of the Spirit of God.

Avoid the Holiday
Tug-of-War

As I WRITE THIS chapter, my wife and I are aboard a 747 on our way to a Christmas vacation at Waikiki Beach, Hawaii. We will be there eight days, to December 29. They have just shown *Herbie Goes to Monte Carlo* as the plane's movie. Jessie and I did not need to see the flick. We had already seen it twice with two of our grandkids. So we did not pay $2.50 for the ear phones for *Herbie.*

Why are we going to Hawaii? Partly to get out of the way of another set of grandparents, my son-in-law's parents. No, "our kids" did not ask us to get lost. In fact, they protested mildly. And no, we do not dislike the other set of grandparents. The truth is, we admire them and appreciate them. They are fine, wholesome people with few flaws and many solid virtues, and an ability to have fun.

Jessie and I, however, live in the same city with our only daughter and son-in-law and three grandchildren, and get to be with them every week, even took two of our grandchildren away to a camp where I was speaking, for a week this past summer. That was one of the times when we saw *Herbie*.

Why shouldn't we clear the grounds for the other set of grandparents? And why shouldn't the grandchildren have time to spend with them at Christmas. After all, they live two states away and do not see their son or this set of grandchildren very often.

DON'T BE A HORRIBLE EXAMPLE

As a counselor every year at holiday time I see some horrible examples of in-laws who offer problems about who stays where, when, and how long.

The most common type of mistake is when one or both sets of parents insist on having the young family visit them at holiday time. This is especially true at Christmas. After all, that is "the time when we all get together."

The next most common problem takes place when the parents of one of the children (the grandparents) decide to visit the young family for the holidays.

One such set of parents who retired to another state insists on staying three weeks in the home of one of their children.

This is the case of two very fine, wholesome, generous people who come seven hundred miles to visit their three sets of children whom they moved away from when they retired farther south. One set of children, my clients, have a large house and are better off financially than the other sets of children. My clients both work, and they have three children—two in the teen years. During the Christmas holidays their home becomes headquarters for the visiting parents.

I said to the man: "Well, Jane tells me her folks are descending on you for a three-week Christmas vacation. How do you feel about that?"

His face fell but he tried to be noble. "We ought to be grateful. They stayed six weeks last year. You understand I like her folks and we get along fine usually. Well, her mother does have one big fault. When she goes anywhere, she takes over—the kitchen, the housecleaning, the wash, and everything anybody in the house does. We can't go anywhere without explaining to her where we are going. I had to tell her off last year when she went too far with one of our teenagers."

"Do they spend the whole time with you and your family?" I asked.

"Oh no," he said, relieved. "They spend time with my wife's brother and sister and their families. But they are home with us every night. They stay in our basement every night. We have more room than the other children, but one of our teenagers gives up his space in the basement. We don't mind, if her mother would not tell us how to run our lives."

His further account, confirmed by his wife, revealed that her mother, a very sacrificial woman, feels that because she "puts out" so thoroughly for everyone, that she has the right to ask very personal questions, give precise advice, and issue appropriate warnings. Most of us know the type.

She plays the "Look How Much I Love You Game." Everybody feels like saying, "Don't love me so much and ask me fewer questions." But this type never gets the message until you verbally black their eyes. Then they have a "Pity Party," acting utterly surprised that they were so grossly misunderstood in their philanthropy and generosity. This type usually says one of two things: "How could you think that I am trying to control you?" Or, "You know that I love you so much; that is the reason I tell you these things." The only answer to such people is, "Don't!" "Don't do it!" Reasoning with this type of manipulator does little good. They are not acting on rationality.

Most of the horrid examples of in-law problems could be avoided if only we would remain as sensible about our interpersonal relations at home as we do at work. It seems that at work, or at the club, or with neighbors, we know that we must be respectful, not make insinuating remarks, avoid blaming other people, control our tempers and resentments, and leave one another free to make decisions without guilt feelings. But this is when we are rational.

For example, "What are your plans for Thanksgiving?" may mean an implied, "You are going to come to see us, aren't you?" or a half dozen other sentences: "You aren't going to see that other set of relatives again this year?"

"You wouldn't leave us lonesome to see our grandkids again this year?"

"You have always come to our place on Thanksgiving, so you wouldn't change the custom this year?"

"You know how his mother is; she always tries to pig the show at Christmas and Thanksgiving."

"The rest of the family is coming this year; you wouldn't disappoint them, would you?"

On the other hand, to ask where a couple will spend Thanksgiving may mean: "We try to make our plans ahead of time so give us some idea where you are going, so we can keep from disappointing anyone. If you, for any reason (even one you do not wish to state) are not coming our way, we will understand. Whatever you do, feel free. Don't come our way unless you both agree on it. We will make our plans after we hear from you."

ONE FAMILY I KNOW ABOUT

Mary and Jack are in a seminary, training to be foreign missionaries, but haven't told their folks for sure. They are training for the pastorate so far as either set of parents knows.

They had to get married. They are both from a small town of three thousand people, belonged to the same church, and married while they were juniors in the same denominational college. Now they have two children, a boy and a girl. The girl came first. With some help from his parents, who run a hardware business in their home town, they are getting along fairly well financially. Otherwise, they are happy; they love each other, adore their children, and are both equally committed to the mission field, if that works out.

The trouble started in planning for the wedding. His mother felt that her mother did not have the social finesse and experience that she had. Consequently, she offered too many suggestions about the wedding, and even offered through her son to bear part of the expense; after all, they had more money—her father was only a carpenter. They went to the same church, mind you.

There were some hard feelings in connection with the wedding, especially concerning the new car which his father gave them for a wedding gift. Unspoken resentments seem to smolder, but "good Christians do not wrangle," so whatever hurt feelings were present were hidden. After all, they attended the same church on Sunday.

Now two children, and four years after the wedding, Christmas is coming. As every year, Mary and Jack are returning to their small town. One problem though.

Each year there has arisen the problem of which set of parents to stay with. Both have adequate homes to take care of them. Jack's family operates more like a clan. They come for miles around on Christmas Day. The family is important. Even Uncle Jeff and his childless, but wealthy, wife fly in from a distant city.

Mary's mother is better with young children, however. After all, she had three. Mary is the oldest of two girls, and there is a boy, six.

Jack's mother has her own viewpoint. She really acts

like she has the divine right to tell Mary and Jack what to do. Look what we have done for you since you have been married, meaning financially, seems to have been her unwritten and unspoken attitude.

The first year was fairly peaceful. They stayed at Mary's folks.

The second year Jack's father, at his mother's instigation he was sure, had a talk with Jack. Was he the head of his house or wasn't he? He even quoted Scripture. It was time Jack put his foot down and let the Jones' (not Mary's folks' real name) know that he was the leader in his family.

Jack pressured Mary into staying with his folks, or at least making their headquarters there. After all, the whole town knew that his folks were largely supporting them in school. And the town, with its intense reconnaissance, as small towns sometimes maintain, knew that Mary and John had to get married, or at least suspected what they did not know for sure. After all, there were some calendar dates to be reconciled.

So they headquartered the second year at Jack's folks. The third year at Mary's. That was okay. Now the fourth year was coming up. Jack and Mary had worked hard at school. There was a three-week break. They needed a vacation. Remember that Mary's mother is excellent with young children; besides, Mary trusts her mother to care for her children; they use the same methods. Besides, Mary needs relief from two young children. Her doctor had told her so. But it is their year to headquarter at Jack's folks. They would not understand, both Jack and Mary agreed.

Hogwash! Baloney! Some will say. Let the young couple stay where they wish. Jack brought this up to his mother just before they went back to school in the fall. They had decided when they came back at Christmas that he and Mary and the children should stay at Mary's folks so her mother could keep the children and give them (Mary and Jack) a chance to be with their friends more, even get away to a nearby large city. After all, it had been a rough fall in the seminary for both of them.

Jack's mother's attitude was that not for a moment would she agree to that arrangement. Right was right. They had stayed with her folks last year. Besides, she could take care of two children if they wanted to get away.

Fortunately, Jack and Mary were together in their viewpoints. They wanted Mary's mother to care for the kids while they were away, and they agreed that they needed to get away. They also agreed that they wanted to headquarter this Christmas at her mother's. But how were they to buck his mother?

At this point, they sought the advice of a counselor who was also a grandfather. As they thought through their rights to make their own decision, the possible consequences, and available ways to break the news to both sets of parents—even the likelihood of it creating a chill in this small church after the facts become clear—they concluded that they had a right to be assertive. The counselor, as is often the case, wasn't there to face with them the consequences of their decision. Let's hope that their Christian understanding of the rights of adult individuals, even of relatives, and the goodwill of the Christmas season combined to make peace on earth in that little town, and in their church.

MY MOST HORRID EXAMPLE

Now for the worst example I know of concerning a tug of war among relatives.

Jenny Sue was an only child. She married, lost her father, and had a baby within a year. Her father had been a very strong and highly-respected dentist. His sudden death by a heart attack did not devastate Jenny Sue's mother, who had a demanding profession of her own to turn to.

Jenny Sue's husband, Steve, was reared by a very manipulating mother who became more erratic in her domineering attitudes as he plowed through adolescence. He survived being reared by a mother and no father. In a way he was glad to have a mother-in-law whom he could respect, as he had not been able to respect his own mother. They all went on vacations together on three different occasions. Jenny Sue's mother became a built-in baby-sitter and loved every minute of it.

However, several things happened, a little at a time. Jenny Sue's mother was able to lavish material things on the young family. Soon Steve became threatened. He asked her to cut back on the spending. He was doing better in his jobs and felt he should buy things for his wife and two girls. Jenny Sue reasoned with her mother, urged her to build a life of her own. After all, she was only fifty. Jenny Sue encouraged her to take trips, join clubs—anything but focus exclusively on her family.

But her mother had "ear trouble." She would not hear Steve nor Jenny Sue. Since Steve had some strength too, a power struggle ensued. Jenny Sue was caught in the middle. Finally, she and Steve outlined a program. Mother was not to give the children anything unless she cleared it with Steve and Jenny Sue. She was not to come over unless she called; she could not barge in unannounced. And they had decided to go on a vacation alone, with the children. Mother's "ear trouble" got worse. Only now she began to flex her muscles and leave presents on the porch for the children. Every special occasion—Easter, Fourth of July, Halloween, and all the others—became a spending spree for Mother.

The showdown came when desperate Steve said to Jenny Sue, "It's me or your mother; I am not going to spend the rest of my life fighting your mother." Jenny Sue got the point. Another baby was on the way. How was she to get across to her hard-headed mother that she did not want her at the hospital when the baby was born, nor her help when she returned home? Her mother seemed to get the message. They let her see the baby but permitted no presents, and no return to the procedure of visiting at any time. They thought mother had changed.

Christmas came soon after the birth of child number three. Mother left extravagant gifts on the front porch. Steve and Jenny Sue sent them back. Mother had them sent back by taxi; Steve and Jenny Sue refused to receive them but paid the taxi driver to return them. It was sad.

After four or five counseling interviews, the mother admitted that she had helped bring on this problem and that it would never become better until she convinced her daughter and son-in-law that she would leave them free to call the shots. Steve and Jenny Sue would not come in for counseling, even for one visit. The mother, however, would not write them a letter saying that from here on she would leave them free to make their own decisions and to define their ways of relating to her. I guess the grandchildren were confused by the whole mess.

Don't Play the Tug-of-War Game

It must be evident by the above examples that two or more people must be involved in tugs of war. Whether they involve verbal dueling or fights to the finish, one person or one side can stop the contest anytime he or she is big enough to. It takes two to play games, whether cards, or contests between relatives. Just refuse. Don't respond. Don't get resentful. Even avoid having a viewpoint if that is the only way to avoid a contest. *Nolo contendere* is the legal phrase, I believe.

When it comes to holidays, vacations, special occasions, even trumped-up visits, families can avoid real sorrow, heartaches, family feuds, misunderstandings, and various family confusions if a few simple rules are observed. Between relatives, in-laws, outlaws, grandparents, estranged and divorced parents, and even between friends, these rules are apropos:

1. Say, write, or send up precise smoke signals that say in "I sentences" what you wish. "We sentences" may hang someone up on an obligation. "Let's sentences" have built in demands. "You sentences" can lead to forthright objection and belligerence.

Level with friends and relatives. Only you know what you feel, wish, or think; this is why the "I" sentences are important. I think, I would like, I had rather, I wish, I don't wish to, I refuse to, I do not like—these are good ways to get the communication show on the road.

2. Check out what others wish to do or plan to do. Do you have your plans yet for vacation? Are you interested in? Where will you be at such-and-such a time? . . . the reason I am asking is that we have been thinking. . . . How do you feel about so-and-so? Before I ask I want you to know our plans are in the windwork (talking about) stage, not the blue print stage. These are good parts of a dialogue that may be successful.

3. If someone's plans change, don't make a federal case out of it. There is never just one way to have a good time or to enjoy a holiday season. Let yourself be creative.

I knew a young couple with three children who had never enjoyed Christmas alone. Her parents, whom they both loved, always came to see them. But one Christmas the parents (grandparents of the three) decided to go on a Mediterranean cruise. (Grandparents do have rights of their own.) Their children and grandchildren were crestfallen. For the first time in fifteen years, they would celebrate Christmas by themselves.

Even though their traditional holiday plans had changed, with a little creativity, that Christmas turned out to be a memorable and enjoyable occasion. Being Christians, more active than her parents, they read the Christmas story from Luke's Gospel on Christmas Eve, and they invited a national from India, who was attending the local university, to spend Christmas Day with them.

4. Finally, never ask *why* when other people tell you their plans. Why is one of the most confusing and guilt producing words in our language. Almost invariably it has a built-in accusation. It causes the same reactions as phrases like, "What do they mean by that?" or "What made them say that?"

Why is God's department. People do not know why they do things, so why ask them? Besides, the question of why almost always means that I have judged this act and do not make sense out of it. Or how could they do that to us?

Come now, it is grandiose to think that you always have to explain human behavior. You can live with puzzlement or ambiguity if you will join the human race and get off Mt. Olympus.

The key is to realize that our children and our other relatives do not belong to us. They have their lives and we have ours. If they do not fit into our formats, we should rejoice. They are being themselves. In the case of our children, we probably helped rear them to be whole persons.

The trick is in *not* reacting to injustice. After all, who is to decide what is unjust? If people act in a manner that seems unfair to us, is that not between them and their Creator?

> Every one of us, then, will have to give an account of himself to God. So then, let us stop judging one another. . . . When someone serves Christ in this way, he pleases God and is approved by others. . . . Happy is the person who does not feel guilty when he does something he judges is right! (Rom. 14:12–13, 18, 22, TEV).

Get Off
Your Rocker

A GREAT GERMAN POET, Friedrich von Schiller, said, "Man is never so entirely human as when he plays." When he plays he is not trying to get new customers, get himself elected to an office, or get a promotion.

John Dewey in a classic of American education memorabilia, *How To Think,* talks about "playfulness" as an attitude of mind and imagination that is very necessary to the good life. A child is free when he plays, free to make a broom into a horse and a chair into a locomotive.

And psychologist Charlotte Buhler points out that the person over sixty returns to what she calls the "pleasure function" of childhood, with no purpose in his behavior other than to enjoy the act of what he is doing. Although it has no purpose, this is one of the ways that older people stay healthy and continue to grow as individuals.

In play the mature years and childhood rightly meet.

What a pity that some grandparents have not heard of this! They might unwind, get out of their rockers, and get involved with children, preferably their own and others' grandchildren.

So often a couple, or a single parent, will say to one set of grandparents, or frequently to a grandmother, "Will you keep the children while we . . . go to a show . . . or camping . . . to take a float trip . . . or even a vacation?"

Unimaginative grandparents take this to mean, keep them from killing each other, feed them, bed them down, and see that they are bathed and their teeth are brushed. So they "watch after them" and feel generous and maybe righteous. They have relieved the parent or parents of the responsibility of caring for the children although the child does nothing but glue himself/herself to the TV, with no censorship of the programs watched. Feeding, bedding, bathing, and just being there is not enough.

Two Basic Errors

Passivity on the part of grandparents is faulty, but two other patterns are even worse.

One is promising the grandchild something that is not delivered. A child from the very early months is building what Erik Erikson called "basic trust." No amount of selling or verbal assurance can create this quality in a child, only explicit description of what to expect and careful living up to that description. It is well known to religious workers that delinquents who had untrustworthy and inconsistent fathers (the same applies to grandfathers) have a hard time believing in God our Father. They got let down in infancy and childhood, or misunderstood what the adults meant, and they assume the universe is run the same way.

A similar error frequently made by grandparents, especially grandfathers, is the sudden cessation of play. One child said, "When my grandfather would play with me he would suddenly say 'That's all, I have to go now;' I didn't know if I had done something wrong or what had happened, so I just looked puzzled and tried to find something else to do." Young children do not comprehend the spread of things or the flow of circumstances well enough to have a category to put such sudden behavior in. It would be much better to say, "Johnny, I will play one round of miniature (putt-putt) golf; that's all the time I have now." Or "After this next round, in about fifteen minutes, I have to go to the store."

There are many positive aspects that might be formulated into rules, but rules are not as important as common sense in coming up with answers about how to make play effective.

A favorite game of my two grandkids, ages ten and twelve, is "Let's drown Grandpa." This, in a pool not too deep, consists of my lying on the bottom of the pool face down while both of them stand on my back. As I need air I flip over upsetting their stance.

Another is "Let's steal his writing pens." I usually have two or three in my shirt pocket. Sometimes I have to make threats of breaking every bone in their bodies if they do not return them immediately from wherever they have hidden them. If their parents are around they may come to my rescue. Or there's the game of "Let's untie Gramps' shoe laces." Roughhousing is not appropriate in some families, but in ours it is one of the games we play.

It is not important what games are played with grandchildren, providing the games are on their level, that they can win some of the time, there is no appreciable danger, and a good time is had by all. Middle age or older grandparents have often schooled themselves in doing something useful, and play seems to be a waste of time. But play is useful for sheer enjoyment.

It might be helpful to think of types of games that we may play with our grandchildren.

Body Movement Games

When children are babies before long they respond to the surprise of peek-a-boo (face alternately covered and uncovered), they respond to stroking and patting and hugging. Then, by the time they are walking, to sit astride of the top leg when one leg is crossed over the other and chant "Trot a little horsey, trot to town; trot a little horsey, don't fall down" with a sudden downward movement, yet holding to both of the child's hands, may please the child very much. Before long you can get into the "hide and seek" routine which may last for years. In fact they outgrow it usually because they are ashamed to play children's games any longer.

By that time you can move on to toss-the-ball, badminton, tennis; the kinds of body-movement games proliferate, depending on what section of the country you are in and what is fashionable in games. Frisbee and throwing or batting balls may be done by someone who is not ambulatory enough to play both ends of the game—e.g., you can throw a frisbee without catching it in return.

When the grandparent does not wish, for health reasons, to participate equally with a grandchild, he/she may set up the game and furnish transportation to the park or seashore or tennis court. Such participation in camping or fishing, without having to exert yourself very much, is the way many grandparents have been a delight to their grandchildren, taught them a lot, and added to the richness of their storehouse of memories. A trip into the woods or a camping trip planned by grandparents, loved and reacted to by all, may fill a whole room in the memory mansion of a grandchild's mind long after we are pushing up roses.

TABLE GAMES

Table games are probably the easiest pastime that most people have access to. It is not difficult to find games that people of all ages will enjoy. And they are not expensive. Hearts. Authors. Rook. Crazy Eight. Kings in the Corner. Monopoly. Checkers. Chinese Checkers. Chess. Dominoes. Scrabble. The list could be extended almost indefinitely. A similar sort of game, Jacks, is played on a hard surface, but you have to be agile enough to sit flat on the floor or ground. These games are played one on one or up to six together, but usually not more than four.

There is even a bonus effect for the adults who play, especially if they have reached the age where walking or running is inexpedient or impossible. Let me give an example.

A few years ago, when I wrote a column for a number of religious papers, a sixty-eight-year-old judge wrote me asking for help. His pathetic story included the fact that he had been a teacher of an adult Bible class for forty years and on the judge's bench for almost the same number of years. Now he is paralyzed from the waist down, is in a wheel chair, and his doctor says he will not walk again. He is deeply depressed and at times obsessed with thoughts of suicide.

I recommended, among other things, that he find someone to play something with and that he invest in his hands—something to keep him from being so much inside himself. If nothing else, he could put a jigsaw puzzle together, but preferably with someone other than himself.

He found a ten-year-old boy next door who was honored and delighted to play checkers with him. It was summer and school was out. They had a great time. Soon the old judge was pulling out of his depression. He had done something about his problem other than feel helpless. And the boy, of course, was getting some grandfathering, close to home.

When older people allow themselves to learn to play, to relate to children, there is something within us senior citizens which reacts well to what seems so natural to junior citizens. I suppose that in every adult, of whatever age, there is within him/her the child he/she once was. We need, for our sakes and our grandchildren's, to turn our inner child out to play. Interacting with grandchildren in table games is a good setting for such enjoyable experiences.

CONSTRUCTION GAMES

Another type of play with children, particularly at various early ages, is building something. Adolescents are less likely to allow us to guide them in their construction impulses, unless we are fortunate enough to have a woodwork shop or a body shop or some special skill that is our avocation (they will probably rebel against it if it is our vocation). But little children like to construct things, whether it's placing blocks on top of each other and knocking them down, or putting tinker toys together to make windmills and numerous other adult-looking projects. Erector set games are a good start for the creative impulses of little geniuses—and most of us grandparents secretly suspect that our grandchildren are something special.

The other set of grandparents of my grandchildren have some distinctive skills that our grandchildren are working to take advantage of. The other grandfather, for example, has a woodwork shop and some tools which do some pretty fancy things with a lathe. My granddaughter, age twelve, has already asked her other grandfather to show her how and to guide her in putting a design on a piece of wood. She already has her design in mind. It will be a peak experience if it comes out well.

There is something thrilling about creativity. Maybe it is an expression of the image of God which the Genesis story and many other passages in the Bible refer to. We are not only rulers over His creation. We are born to be creators, to come up with new ways of doing something, to be innovators. That is why a pair of fresh eyes are so needed in playing or living.

If grandparents can assist in creativity, the child will build a bridge between play and work. It does not matter whether the content of creativity is designing a doll's clothes, making up a clown's face, building a bird house or playing an electronic game, the process and enthusiasm and satisfaction are what matter. And speaking of electronic games, we are on the verge of having games which will acquaint children with what is certainly the most characteristic development of our time, computers. Calculators are already widely used. And computer games for the masses are just around the corner.

WIT GAMES

Wit is used in the Old English sense of knowing, understanding, being alert mentally, and in the modern sense of the comic or the humorous. Games that test our knowledge and at the same time are fun employ both uses of the word *wit*. The aspect of puzzlement—surprise, outwitting the other person, forcing ourselves or others to figure out answers—and even the exhibitionist aspect of winning are all a part of what causes us to smile or belly laugh or relax in sheer satisfaction of seeing the goal arrived at. Many games use our minds and tickle our funny bones at the same time.

My granddaughter tried this mental puzzle out on me: "A man was found hanging from the light fixture in an empty room in which there was no furniture. There was a carpet on the floor which had a large wet spot on it.

How did he hang himself?" After I tested my wits over that for awhile and flunked, she said gleefully, "He stood on a huge ice cube." Then she sprung this one on me: "Adam and Eve and Pinch-me went down to the river to bathe. Adam and Eve got drowned, which one of the three was saved?" I didn't know until I said, "Pinch-me" that her fingers could pinch so hard.

There are all sorts of riddles and mental puzzles and tongue twisters and challenging games. Consult your public library or book store.

But if you are traveling and want to avoid the "Gramp, how much further? How long will it be until we get there?" You can watch the signs on the highway and play the Alphabet game:

"I see an A."

"I see a B in that 'Be Prepared' sign, and a D and E."

"Hold it, that wasn't a good word; you left out C."

"Oh yeah, that's right. Okay, I'll see a C soon. They are easy to find."

The one who gets farthest in the alphabet is the winner. But don't be surprised if you have a hard time finding Q or X or Z.

If they tire of that, you can try collecting license plates. Of course, if you are driving you will have to appoint a secretary to write down the states you see. He can help you look too, and that will put you two against however many there are in the car, which they will notice with a loud clamor.

Whether traveling or sitting at home, "Twenty Questions" always challenges our wits. One says, "I have something in my mind. . . ." Question: "Is it fowl, fish, or plant?" The leader may say, "Fowl." Question one: "Does it fly to get its food?" Or "Does it make its nest in a tree usually?" The questions continue until someone guesses the correct answer. Then he/she becomes "it" and gets to lead.

Then there are all sorts of physical puzzles which may be found in toy or specialty shops. Work them yourself first, which may take a lot of doing, and give the grandkid whatever coaching is needed to keep it from being too difficult. Then watch the challenge and the fun.

If you run out of everything else, you can always pick up a *Guinness Book of World Records* and one or more can play a guessing game. It will be a test of general knowledge to see how close each one can get to the facts. A *World Almanac* may be used the same way. Or if you have a light portable dictionary, a "spelling bee" may be enjoyable at home or on a trip.

The important fact is that any grandparent, of whatever educational level, can find something playful to do with grandchildren—something that's mind developing, mind boggling, or just plain fun. It all depends on how grandparents see their role, as baby-sitter, guide, promoter, coach, or interesting friend. It can be a delightful role, but it is basically what we make it.

Two social scientists at the University of Chicago, Bernice L. Neugarten and Karol K. Weinstein studied seventy sets of grandparents. They listed five types: (1) The Formal grandparent, (2) The Fun-seeking grandparent, (3) The Surrogate-parent grandparent, (4) The Reservoir-of-Family-Wisdom grandparent, (5) The Distant-figure grandparent. Most of us play all these roles at times. But if I had to choose one that has the greatest possibilities for making a lasting contribution to everyone concerned, and one that may enhance the other roles, it would be the Fun-seeking grandparent. With the information that is turning up these days on the importance of laughter and the value of peak experiences in healthy and happy living, we who teach our grandchildren to enjoy life may be making a greater contribution to them, even to their physical health, than we know.

Besides, it seems to me that this represents our religion

better than what I hear from some "middle-escent" and senescent friends who say that the world is going to the dogs and you can't trust anybody, even relatives. People who learn to laugh at some things will probably find fewer things to cry about. Laughter distinguishes us from all other creatures (the laughing hyena isn't really tickled). And Henri Bergson was probably right when he wrote that laughter is "the corrective force which prevents us from becoming cranks."

Someone wrote a Southern editor once and asked if he thought Jesus Christ ever laughed. He replied, "I don't know whether or not Jesus ever laughed; I suspect He did, but I can tell you one thing: He fixed me up so that I could." Hooray! Olé! Laughter is a lot better than ho-hum.

When death comes prowling around my house I'd like for my grandchildren to see me grin him right back into the shadows.

In the meantime, it is important that the family learn to play together as well as pray together. Therefore, I would like to suggest, as bold as it may seem, that grandparents try to observe the following ten guidelines when your grandchildren honor you by sharing themselves with you:

1. Don't act silly and try to be another child. They had rather have time with you as the adult that you are.

2. Don't condemn them for being bad losers. You probably were too at their age.

3. Enjoy working or playing with them. Don't just be an observer.

4. Don't moralize. Simply state the facts about how reality is.

5. When they want an audience, be one. "Watch me" and "look at me" are good reminders coming from a child.

6. Play their games. They may be better than yours. "Kick the can" may be what they want to do now.

7. Be a good sport. If they beat you, they beat you. Play honestly and the best you can.

8. It's all right to brag on them to their face, provided it is true.

9. Use your imagination. They may like your ideas for work or play.

10. Talk to kids. Ask them what they think and what they like and where they wish to go. They may tell you.

Be a Self-Esteem
Generator

IT IS NOW KNOWN that the most important asset any human being has is a good feeling about himself—not just a good self-image nor a healthy self-concept. It is how you feel about you as a person, how you value yourself, how healthily you love yourself, how accurately you appraise your worth as a human being. After all, God didn't make any junk.

We have just passed through the "me decade," as Tom Wolfe called it. Narcissism has been spilling all over the place, even in the sanctuaries. But the need for healthy self-esteem, which includes humility not humiliation, is here to stay.

The New England poet, Henry Wadsworth Longfellow, hinted at one of the functions of self-esteem in his poem, "Michael Angelo":

He that respects himself is safe from others;
He wears a coat of mail that none can pierce.

And he could have said that such a self-respector feels
good enough about himself to remove his coat of mail
and become vulnerable at times—that is also true.

By the time you are old enough to be a grandparent,
forty-five and up generally, you realize that this is a rough
old world—and this is not old folks' talk (senile-ese)—it
is simple fact. We can't help but wonder as we look at
our grandchildren or great grandchildren what they will
do with the "times that try men's souls." They may say,
"God be thanked Who has matched us with [this] hour"
(Rupert Brooke) or "The time is out of joint; O cursed
spite that ever I was born to set it right" (Shakespeare).
Or will they just say "the world is my oyster" and start
gobbling it down?

My thesis here is that the grand function of grandparents
is to be self-esteem generators. If self-esteem is the key
to successful coping in any individual's life or to transcending into greatness, as I believe it is, the function of parents
and grandparents and teachers and doctors and minis-
ters, and even great-grandparents is to create the kind
of situations where self-esteem can grow and become
the warp or woof—the very fabric—of the rising generation.

Baby-sitting, taking children on vacations, buying toys
or cars for grandchildren are incidental and a means to
the end. The end is Christian character, concern for others,
awareness of their own finitude, and an ever-expanding
inner self. It is inevitably related to whether they see
themselves as the unique and important selves who are
worth self-cultivation. Even Rabelais, in the sixteenth
century, saw that "So much is a man worth as he esteems
himself."

"HOW NOT TO" BUILD SELF-ESTEEM

John Milton was not far off center when he wrote

> Oft times nothing profits more
> Than self-esteem, grounded on just and right.

Milton may have had a moralistic connotation in mind. Today we would tend to talk in terms of what is rational, reality orientation, what is self-defeating behavior, or that which keeps us from being self-actualized. But we are dealing with the same content. What a person sows he still tends to reap, and "wild oats" still make a lousy breakfast, permissiveness or no permissiveness.

The situation is so bad with some grandparents that one pediatrician, Lewis A. Coffin, M.D., who was especially interested in the dietary problems of children, wrote a book called *The Grandmother Conspiracy* (Santa Barbara: Capra Press, 1974). He says: "As soon as a person becomes a grandparent, he or she undergoes a radical personality change—stern fathers become cooing grandfathers; harpie-type mothers melt and crawl on the floor, sing lullabies and cram cookies and cookies and cookies down their sweet little grandchildren's throats, take them to the ice-cream store, bake cakes and pies for them, and stand back admiringly as the little ones swell, tweak their obese little cheeks approvingly, and raise a terrible hue and cry if anyone tries to interfere" (p. 10).

Dr. Coffin may or may not be carried away about the harm of excess sugar and other carbohydrates, but he is certainly talking about some grandparents I have known. They, by some strange quirk of mistaken reasoning, think they are helping children by allowing them to spend money unwisely, waste unnecessary hours in front of TV, jump up and down on beds or sofas (which they are not allowed to do at home); in short, they allow them to get by with anything except murder. So parents tell me, "It take us two or three weeks to straighten the children out after a visit of several days at their grandparents."

And what will these children think of their grandparents later when reality stares them in the face from so many avenues. They will wonder if the sappy, sentimental, self-indulgent attitudes of their grandparents were really the best that they (the grandparents) knew. "We can wrap Gramp around our little finger when we want to" said by grandchildren is no compliment to the grandfather.

On the other hand, when grandchildren do make honest mistakes, goof, or show the holes in their learning or experience, it does not help their self-esteem to put them down, laugh at them, or show them up unmercifully. After all, all of us have blind spots in our knowledge and generally hold devoutly to some blatant errors. Frequently our self-esteem depends on defending our ignorance.

For example, in a family conversation in the presence of my very bright grandson I made a reference to the novel *Lord of the Flies*. He had heard his older sister talk of J. R. R. Tolkien's popular, *Lord of the Rings*. It suddenly occurred to him that he had one on me, so with a great outburst of laughter he said, "Gramp, you said *Lord of the Flies;* it's *Lord of the Rings.*" I hate a smart-aleck kid! You see, I was never allowed to correct my grandfather; we were carefully schooled on the subject of respecting our elders. Rather impulsively I said, "Nicky, you are making a fool of yourself. Ten years ago, William Golding, an English novelist, wrote a novel that is now considered a classic. It is called *Lord of the Flies.* Don't laugh about things you don't know anything about."

I could have done better than that. It is so easy to put a child down. Sometimes we need to commend them for their efforts, even when the results are not perfect. When my wife or I get critical over some little thing, our grandchildren will say, "Hey, don't get so hyper; it's not that important." And they are often right.

Take, for example, the grandchild who breaks something valuable, or misplaces a tool, or loses something for which there is no excuse (according to your middle-age or super-annuated mind). How do you handle such a crisis? Shall we, grandparents, overlook the incident, act like nothing happened, be the all-forgiving and all-accepting grandparent? If we do, any average grandchild will see the phoniness and unrealism of our seeming munificence. Later they will wonder why we did not have the good sense to see that tough love is just as important as tender love. If the child's errors or even faux pas were normal for his/her age we should console him/her and take steps to prevent a recurrence of the event. If they were willfully destructive, the logical consequences of such behavior should be made clear, and the next time they should be held entirely accountable. It increases a child's self-esteem to know that adults (including grandparents) love them enough to set limits and to expect them to be responsible—in the long run, at least.

Now, on the positive side, how can grandparents contribute to the growing up and the development of normally self-respecting and self-directing adult human beings? Grandparents, like parents who know what they are doing, aim at working themselves out of a job, producing children who will not need them, or who will move from asking them what to do, and become sincere friends who may or may not talk over their sorrows and joys with them.

How Self-Esteem Can Be Built

If some ivory tower researcher were to look back through history in various cultures, he/she would likely find that older people have usually transmitted both good and bad influences through three mediums: examples, tales which embody values, and slogans or wise sayings.

In an earlier chapter, I dealt with the example of parents and grandparents, and the importance of consistency between them and with other influential factors (teachers, Scout leaders, etc.).

The critical problems arise when there is a wide diversity in the lifestyles, or values, or language habits between the families involved.

One grandparent said to me, "What do people expect me to do when these kids come to my house? The other set of grandparents eat like pigs at the table, cuss like sailors, and have no respect for the church and religion. I cannot stand for the kids to use bad language at my house."

"You are up against something bigger than you can change, aren't you?"

"Yes, but what am I expected to do?"

"What about picking out two or three things that you think they might do differently and (after you have made your pattern clear, that 'we do it this way at our house') expect their cooperation. Then reward them, brag on them, thank them, or even give them a financial reward. Make good behavior pay off. All psychologists are agreed on this. But don't expect reform on too many fronts."

You see, we are so prone to relying on explaining "good" behavior, lecturing, criticizing, and even condemning bad behavior, that it is difficult for us to believe in the power of a wholesome example. It means essentially that we doubt the effectiveness of grace, of gracious behavior. Jesus must have thought that example was a powerful motivator of change. Twice before his death he said to his disciples, "This is my commandment, that you love one another as I have loved you" (John 15:12; also see 13:34).

The best antidote to the bad influence of a bad son-in-law, a careless daughter-in-law, or even another set of pagan grandparents is to be a beautiful, loving, valuable, compassionate Christian.

And here is the answer to the question about what to do in the face of conflicting standards and values and lifestyles. But it is not an easy answer—at least, not for me—because it requires so much of me.

Shakespeare has a character in *The Merchant of Venice* who says it perfectly:

> If to do were as easy as to know what were good to do, chapels had been churches and poor men's cottages princes' palaces. It is a good divine that follows his own instructions; I can easier teach twenty what were good to be done, than be one of the twenty to follow mine own teaching. The brain may devise laws for the blood, but a hot temper leaps o'er a cold decree.

When we have worked hard and even tortured ourselves in getting where we are, learning "what were good to do," it is sometimes saddening to see our "instructions" ignored or sabotaged. So we are stuck with the process of continuing to set a good example, and leave the rest to God and to our offspring.

Every family, too, has its myths, sometimes its mythic heroes. The grandchild at a certain age may trigger off some story by saying (usually sincerely), "Was your grandfather a slave holder?" or "Grandma, did you know your grandmother?" Then the heroic stories begin to spill out.

I remember my parents telling me how one of their grandmothers staved off the advances of the Yankees when they came through raiding the cattle and horses. The story was about one mare named Sal. When a group of soldiers demanded that she give them Ole Sal, she refused. She had saddled the mare and intended to ride off before they arrived, but was surprised and surrounded by a few Union soldiers. One of them tried to pull her out of the sidesaddle while another held the horse. She kicked and screamed and said, "You can shoot me if you wish, but before you take Ole Sal, you will have to kill me first." Her bravery impressed them so and triggered such compassion in the leader of the group that he eventually said, "Let her keep the horse if it means that much to her." They left.

I don't know how much of that story was God's truth, but one little boy sure got the impression that one ancestor had a lot of bravery.

A similar embodiment of virtue was passed on to my grandchildren when one said, "Gramp, do you remember when you first saw an airplane?" That was all I needed.

"Yeah, one flew over our farm. It was a little cub plane. I was about eight years old. It created quite a stir in our community. We were not sure what we were seeing. Certainly no bird was that big and made that much noise. There was a big controversy in the community about whether some people saw an airplane or whether they were just 'seeing things.'

"One old black washwoman who worked for my father's parents when he was growing up, was reported to have said, 'I didn't see it myself and I don't know who to believe whether there really was a plane or not, but I'll tell you one thing, if Mr. Bob (meaning my father) says that he saw it, I'll believe it. I helped raise that young'un and he doesn't lie.' Aunt Sue, as we called her, was right. My father was a fanatic about telling the truth. You never lied to him twice. He would never believe you the second time."

Grandparents, of course, never tell how Aunt Ida was the black sheep of the family, or how Uncle Jordan shot his finger off to keep from getting drafted in World War I, or how Great Grandfather hid out in the mountains to avoid fighting in the Civil War, or who in the family became an alcoholic. Nor should they, I suppose, even though some of these tales would have stood up well with Chaucer's or Truman Capote's.

At least the heroic tales of elegant ancestors serve to add to one's sense of identity and establish a tradition of family values.

Similarly, self-esteem is often enhanced by the "sayings" that are passed on in the family, especially by grandparents. These sayings should be the accumulated wisdom of the past generations which every educator and most parents know is difficult to transmit to the young. Knowledge can be transmitted; wisdom does not easily pass from one generation to another.

Yet cognitive therapists and/or those who subscribe to rational emotive therapy know that man does not live by bread alone, but by slogans and proverbs. If grandparents can state their accumulated wisdom with humility and resist the temptation to pontificate and dogmatize, they may be heard and heeded. Their wisdom must be stated in such terms as, "It seems to me," or "I have often found it to be true," or "I always heard my mom say," or "For whatever it's worth, I think."

There is an interesting similarity between the wisdom sneaked in by some modern psychotherapists and the wisdom transmitted by successful parents and grandparents. For example, either might have said:

"You can't expect everybody to love you."

"If you don't believe in yourself, who will believe in you?"

"Whatever you sow you reap."

"If you haven't learned to fail you haven't learned to live."

The list could be extended indefinitely, as long as the human mind is wide. Wisdom in capsule form may not determine our behavior in all cases, but it helps to bolster our stamina in times of crisis.

Nothing adds to a person's self-esteem as much as a feeling of competence in coping with every phase of life. Parents, grandparents, employers of teenagers, pastors, teachers, all will do well to keep in mind three important factors in generating self-esteem.

RESPECT INDIVIDUALITY

The first important factor in generating self-esteem is respecting the child's individuality.

Someone has said: "Always remember that you are absolutely unique. Just like everyone else." This is important concerning your grandchildren. I met a woman recently who has twenty-three grandchildren and seven great-grandchildren. Refraining from comparing them with one another must be a colossal task. Some must be cuter; others smarter; others very friendly and outgoing. Somehow people seem to sense when you accept them in all of their uniqueness. And it is inspiring and comforting to find one human being of any age, related or unrelated to you by blood, who receives you in all your uniqueness.

The verse from Proverbs, "Train up a child in the way he should go, and when he is old he will not depart from it" (22:6) may be correctly translated, some Bible scholars tell us, "train a child in the way he is," according to his own nature. It is like our word *educate*, from Latin *educere*, to lead out, to draw from within, develop what is really there. Sometimes the grandparents are the only human beings who see a child's uniqueness and are willing for him/her to be exactly according to his/her distinctiveness. Parents may be trying to create carbon copies of themselves or achieve their unfulfilled dreams in their kids, and they may insist that teachers and other guides be a part of this invisible and unrecognized coercion.

When one of my clients was in the process of working through some emotional problems, I asked, "Who was the biggest influence in your growing up? I don't understand who the significant others were. Your father was gone most of the time you say. Your mother ran around with other men and drank a lot. You could not have modeled after her. Who did you look up to?"

"That's easy," she replied. "It was my grandfather and my grandmother. I didn't spend much time with them because my mother hated them. They were daddy's parents. But they loved me and told me so."

"How could they have influenced you much? You say you didn't see them much," I responded.

"Oh, but they believed in me. They made me believe in myself. I remember once my grandfather talked to me and said, 'Ellie, I want to tell you something. You don't have to let your parents' problems ruin you. There is something great in you. There is no telling what you can become. The world out there needs you.' I shall never forget that speech. He made me believe in myself."

What an opportunity we have as grandparents.

Avoid Guilt and Shame

A second factor in motivating and moving children toward their potential is that of using the right stimulators— avoiding guilt and shame.

All of us grandparents hope to be a good influence on the second or third generation behind us. It is a kind of social immorality.

Guilt is the psychic pain, though a dull ache sometimes, that we feel when we think we have let somebody down— God, our family, our friends, or even ourselves. Shame is the loss of face or the embarrassment we feel when significant others know of our failures, or even might know, and we fear their disapproval.

Some families try to rear their children, motivate them to behave or to achieve, by guilt or shame or both. "Don't you know that you are an awful person for doing that!" That's guilt. Or "Aren't you ashamed of yourself; what will people think of us?" That's shame. Both have their hazards so far as sound motivation is concerned.

Parents and grandparents both have to let children know

that some behavior is unacceptable and some approved. We need to distinguish between the behavior and the person. Wouldn't it be more conducive to good long range results if we said things like: "I don't think you will be proud of that behavior later;" or "You are capable of much better behavior than that;" or "I don't understand what you were doing, but I have confidence that you will not keep on; you have too much sense;" or "I know you know that we love you, and we hope you love us enough to straighten up."

Jesus used this love appeal. "If a man loves me, he will keep my word. . . . If a man does not abide in me, he is cast forth as a branch and withers." (John 14:23; 15:6). Grace and truth (John 1:14), that was Jesus' appeal. If we understand "truth" to be reality—the way things really are, that which ultimately must be faced—we have a sound basis for healthy action.

We can build a home on grace and truth, not on law. We can rear children and contribute to the welfare of grandchildren using the cornerstones of grace and truth. We must ask ourselves about our behavior: Is it loving? And, will it get us where we are going, in line with reality? So far in the history of Christianity, there have been few times when Christians have depended completely on grace and truth. They often resort to shaming and punishing and making people feel guilty, which does not do much for self-esteem.

LOOK FOR SUCCESSES

The third factor to keep in mind for generating self-esteem in children is that of looking for their successes.

It is a severe indictment of a parent or grandparent when a child has to say "Don't I ever do anything right?" They are usually aware of doing a good many things wrong. This in itself puts a strain on the child or adolescent's self-esteem. Much of their rebellion and defiance is an attempt to establish an identity, to prove that they are not babies anymore.

What grandchildren need, like what everyone else needs, are some successes. I like to think I do a few things well. Some do well at their jobs. Some are good neighbors and friends. Some cope well with crises, rise to difficult occasions with poise and patience. Some are good church workers. What do your grandchildren do well and who praises them for it?

If there is any one thing child psychologists, pediatricians, and counselors with children agree on, it is: If you want good behavior repeated, reward it, reinforce it by establishing some meaningful payoff. Punishment may be necessary at times. Ignoring certain objectionable behavior, like a child's holding his breath or banging his head against the floor, is sometimes in order. All agree that there should not be a payoff for reprehensible behavior.

But, so often we neglect to plan our relationships with grandchildren so that they get the ego exhilaration of doing something well. It should be something they feel good about. This could be anything: making a cake, playing ball, riding a horse, playing cards, writing a letter, ironing clothes, knowing a lot of facts out of *Guinness Book of Records*. The important criteria for the activity or attainment is that the grandchild feel distinctive about it. Who wants to be mediocre at everything? And who is going to recognize a child when he succeeds and commend him? Remember, if you want good behavior, whether good grades or good ball throwing, someone has to do the reinforcing; there has to be a payoff.

I suppose there must be some children and teenagers who have had too much commendation. They seem cocky or too talkative and assertive. It must be about them that Frank Colby wrote: "Self-esteem is the most voluble of the emotions." But for every one who has an inflated ego,

I can show you one hundred who have been starved emotionally and who long for someone to say some kind words of praise and admiration.

Words like: "You looked good out there on that field." Or "What I like most about you is the way you take defeat; you act real mature about it." Or "I just noticed how well you are writing lately." Or "I guess I am prejudiced because I'm your grandparent, but did you hear the way they cheered you." Or "It must be very satisfying to handle things as well as you did; I was terribly proud of you."

It's true for all of us, parents, grandparents, and certainly grandchildren—we need reinforcement. Our self-esteem needs feeding, over and over. Isn't that worth being thoughtful about?

Here are some rules that may help generate self-esteem:

1. Don't lecture about the need for self-esteem. It is a plant that grows when you are not looking.

2. Set the stage for successes. Find things to do that they can excel at.

3. Be specific about the rules, whether at work or play.

4. Encourage and comfort a grandchild when he/she makes a booboo.

5. Confront them firmly, and sternly if necessary, when they intentionally violate rules.

6. When you compliment, make clear that you do not expect perfection. They may turn a commendation into a mandate.

7. Spend time with your grandchild. This very process of spending time tells them they are worth it.

Let Yourself
Be You

THERE ARE SEVERAL ways to say what I am trying to get across in this chapter.

"Act your age" came to mind. But, really, it has nothing to do with your age, except that as a grandparent likely you are approaching the second half of your stay on this earth. You may even be in your declining years (especially physically, maybe mentally). It is realistic and mature to admit this when it comes up. And don't act as if you have retained all of your youthful qualities and capabilities. Such hypocrisy is not necessary to say the least.

Be mature, keep growing, don't fault yourself at fifty or stall at sixty or turn sour at seventy. The fact is, people do usually stop growing emotionally and spiritually because they are older. This need not be. They get old in mind and attitude because they stop setting new goals and venturing out of their ruts.

The question, then, becomes: How do I keep growing? How do I become the whole me, the authentic self? How do I become assertive enough to be genuine and remain humble enough not to be a problem to my environment? To be me or not to be me, that is the question.

HUMBITION IS THE WORD

Walter Kaufman, a philosophy professor at Princeton, invented the word *humbition*. *Humbition* means having ambition enough to keep reaching toward your full capacity as a human being and humility enough to admit your natural limitations. It is important at any age, but especially as we get older.

In our culture many of us got brainwashed on the subjects of ambition and humility. In childhood we were told, "Don't be vain," or "Don't be stuck on yourself," or "Don't think you are better than other people," or "Don't be conceited." This often meant that we were not to assert ourselves or think well of ourselves, and certainly not to be the best of anything.

Humility, in collaboration with these "don't be" injunctions, came to mean that since we are of the earth, earthly (the root meaning of "humble"), we must necessarily put ourselves down. To be humble was a virtue. So we almost became proud of our humility. Like the man who said, "I used to be conceited and proud before I got religion; now there is not a proud bone in my body."

The Bible was even used as part of this brainwashing— all out of context, of course. For example: Psalm 22:6 said, "I am a worm, and no man." This could make you feel pretty bad. Or the Apostle Paul's word to each one of us, "Not to think of himself more highly than he ought to think" (Rom. 12:3), does not tell us precisely how we ought to feel about ourselves. Jesus helps us greatly when he urges us to remember that the very hairs of our heads are numbered and that we are of more value than the sparrows, not one of which is forgotten of God.

And along came assertiveness training books that told us to say "No" and not feel guilty. Or books that said we have a right to be Number One in our lives, and even to be our own best friend.

Grandparents and grandchildren may have this in common. Both have to assert their authenticity in a world that does not value their common commodity, their market value, or rather their lack of market value. In a society which emphasizes production—how much you can turn out—children are a question mark and may be a drag. They have not yet become productive and may never really succeed. And grandparents may be at the stage in life, or looking toward it, when they are not producers. Both older people and children are living off of society.

Then being—being important in your own right, just because you *are,* is all either young or old has left. That gets down to the bedrock of existence. We must build on the solid rock by saying: "I am me; I am valuable as a person; I must reach for my goals and chart my course; but in the meantime I have the right to value myself as I am, just as I am at any given moment."

EARN YOUR NEIGHBOR'S LOVE

The rub comes when we, as grandchildren or grandparents, decide that we can behave any way we wish and still expect to be loved.

Hans Selye, in his delightful little book, *Stress Without Distress,* has sounded a good note about earning love.

Children and older people often fall into the trap of assuming that we are going to be loved regardless of our performance. Children say or act as if they are saying: "Here I am; I did not ask to be born. Because I am your child, you must love me unconditionally and regardless of my behavior." That is very unrealistic.

Grandparents easily assume: "I have paid my dues to life. Look what sacrifices I have made to rear my children. I deserve my grandchildren's love, time, and respect. I have love coming to me even if I am bossy, cranky, or meddlesome." But as the song says, "It ain't necessarily so."

While we are admitting God's infinite love for us and attempting to love our neighbor as we do ourselves, we (young and old) have to reckon with the hard-nosed facts that if we are going to be loved, we have to get within courting distance of acting in a lovable manner.

Love begets love, unselfishness breeds unselfishness, and forgiveness calls people to forget the past and live intensively in the present and the future. When grandparents set a good example by acting in a manner which evokes respect and admiration and communication, they get all three. When they act as if they have a divine right to be loved, just because they have worked and loved in the past, they will be disappointed.

It seems to be a kind of axiom that *each of us should aim at loving our fellow persons in spite of their failures and foibles, but not expect other persons of any age to love us unless we act in a lovable manner.* This will be a great example to our grandchildren, preached and practiced.

WISE SELFISHNESS

Deserving love or acting in a lovable manner is one thing, but all of us face repeatedly the crucial question of how to find the balance between giving to others and living for ourselves. There are three questions here, the first one already partially answered: How do I deserve love? How do I give love? How do I love myself healthily?

These become important in grandparenting because sometimes our children keep right on expecting us to devote ourselves to their happiness like we did when they were little. And their children, our grandchildren, adopt the same stance: "Ask Grandpa" or "Let Grandmother do it."

I have known grandparents who range all the way from selfish ogres to sacrificial Sams and soft Sallys. The family slave is not a good image for a grandparent. On the other hand, the selfish, self-centered, arrogant, unbending older person—even if passive and not a trouble maker—is a most pathetic figure. "Nobody's gonna turn me into a free, built-in baby-sitter," is one extreme. The other extreme is, "Let me do it; I don't have anything else to do; you know how I love to help." In between is the grandparent who has a life of his/her own, but also has time to take grandchildren to the park or to movies or even to Europe.

The trick is in understanding selfishness and not operating from guilt.

Perhaps it will help if we distinguish between selflessness, selfness, and selfishness. The selfless persons tend to neglect self altogether; they build up deep resentment when gratitude is not returned for love, and they have little life of their own. The selfish person puts self first, expects everything to revolve around himself or herself, and invariably asks, "What do I get out of it?" The person with selfness, a healthy sense of self, realizes that I am responsible for me, that it is not bad for me to look out for my own best interests, and I have a right to reach toward my own potential as a person.

We might deny that we have to or ought to bother about trying to love relatives. Isn't it enough to love our own household or friends—people who love us back? Jesus answers that succinctly in the Sermon on the Mount, "Love your enemies" (Matt. 5:43–48).

Note that Jesus does *not* say "regard your enemies as friends." Sometimes those we love do not have our best interests at heart, and we must recognize them as a kind of enemy in order to protect ourselves. This caution is a kind of wise selfishness.

This is not the same as looking out for *Numero Uno*. It is close, however, to being your own best friend. In fact, it has been observed for years that people who do not know how to love themselves healthily and wisely do a poor job of loving others. They get involved in bribery, loving others with a secret belief that this will get themselves loved in return. Or in trying to appease their own consciences by making up for past failures by present donations of time, good will, or even money.

The only kind of love that does not have built-in tricks for self-defeat is that in which one person loves another simply and sincerely because he or she finds it joyous, and seemingly helpful, to love. You love because you are loving. Or, you act loving because love is in your heart. Whether or not it is returned is another matter.

I Gotta Be Me

In the sixties young people were singing a song which sounded strange to their elders' ears, "I Gotta Be Me."

But those young people had a point. The idea of being yourself is important for any age, anywhere, at any time. Each human being has inalienable, inherent, obvious rights, such as the right of privacy and the right of self-determination. I'm not so sure about the importance of life, liberty, and the pursuit of happiness. Life, yes. Liberty within the limits of other people's rights and in concurrence with my own self-responsibility, yes. But pursuing happiness probably causes it to flee from you. Happiness is a by-product of a person's living for what he/she considers worthwhile—whatever makes life significant.

So what matters is for each of us to set our own goals, chart our own course, and steer our own ships.

For many this will be learning to enjoy life more than we have ever done before. As stated earlier, psychologist Charlotte Buhler speaks of the last period in life as, at its best, being filled with "function pleasure." This means that we spend our time or, at least, a larger portion of it doing things that have no purpose except enjoyment. Like children who play or explore or adventure for the purpose of experiencing. Most of our lives we have been doing things for growth, for pleasing customers, for increasing our reputation, or even out of duty to God.

I am not suggesting that we turn off the church or tune out the call of God. Rather, we might find the best adult maturity by allowing ourselves a healthy second childhood. Just imagine your grandchildren or great-grandchildren saying: "There is something great about the way Grammaw and Grampaw have grown old. We always said that he was a workaholic and that she was determined to play the role of the family slave. Now they do things for sheer fun. They seem to get pleasure out of just living. They play games. They go places together for the heck of it. And they don't seem to be duty driven like they have been all their lives. I hope I can be like that when I get old."

Or if you have freed yourself of some of the compelling obligations of duty and demand, you may even find joy in creativity.

Think of Grandma Moses who was painting real masterpieces in her eighties. Michelangelo was still producing masterpieces at eighty-nine. Goethe completed the second part of *Faust* when he was eighty-two. Longfellow was still writing some of his best poetry after seventy. Voltaire wrote *Candide* at sixty-five and Wagner finished *Parsifal* at sixty-nine. Or to get closer to our day, Bernard Shaw wrote a play at ninety-two. Albert Schweitzer was still head of a large African hospital at eighty-nine. And George Burns won his first Academy Award at age eighty. He says he can't die before the year 2000 because he has scheduled engagements. And there was Lowell Thomas, who died August 29, 1981 at age eighty-nine and who worked the day before "in good spirits"; and Lawrence Welk, who is still going strong on TV every week. This is to say nothing about a few people in every community who have done an equally good job of living life well as long as they breathe and who are a constant source of inspiration to those around them, though largely unhonored by their communities. Maybe we need a Mr. or Ms. Senior Citizen Day or a Medal of Honor for Great Grays.

No wonder Walter Pitkin said in *Life Begins at Forty* that nine-tenths of the world's best work has been done by older people, well past what we call their "prime." So far as admirable living is concerned, our prime may be yet to come. If we really believe that God is living through us and always creating us, the way we live our mature years may become God's miniature masterpiece. Or is that conceit? I enjoy believing that it is realistic and courageously possible.

Browning said it succinctly in "Rabbi Ben Ezra":

> Grow old along with me!
> The best is yet to be,
> The last of life, for which the first was made:
> Our times are in his hand
> Who saith, "A whole I planned,
> Youth shows but half; trust God: see all, nor be afraid!"

One of the fondest images any of us can hope for in our own children or grandchildren is that of our being unassumingly grand. To have them say, "There in this sorry world of ours went a great woman (or a great man)."

It would seem that the best way to leave such a legacy is to be genuine, authentic, self-directing and continuously growing—right down to the mortuary.

So I would like to suggest some guidelines which seem relevant to grandparenting as we continue to be ourselves in spite of whatever ravages and hazards befall us as we experience "the heart-ache and the thousand natural shocks/That flesh is heir to" (Shakespeare). The following questions offer us the opportunity to take a good look at ourselves:

1. Are you acting from within? Is it your decision or are you reacting to other people's foibles, bad behavior, or even to their joys and good behavior? To act is very different from reacting; the former is highly human and mature.

All of us at times have to go along with tradition or attend meetings when we do not wish to. But happy people are those who act responsibly and creatively for themselves in as many areas as possible. We are victims of custom or convention or current agendas only if we allow ourselves to be. We can make our own ways or, like sheep, walk in the paths others have made and spend our lives reacting rather than acting.

2. Can you control your own moods? Or do you allow yourself to become the victim of the moods around you? You can choose your reactions, whether depression or elation, once you assume responsibility for yourself. The Book of Proverbs says, he that rules his own spirit is better than the mighty (16:32). We are prone to say, "I got up blue this morning," or "My anger got the better of me," as if we had no choices in the matter. But the minute we assume responsibility for our blues or our anger or our procrastination, we begin to feel like persons rather than automatons. Unless we are really sick mentally, like having a chemical depression, we can assume a "choice attitude." We can say, "I will do something about my moods," not

"I will think myself out of my problems or read my way to health." Some problems we act our way out of. Crazy or lazy moods are such problems.

3. How do you act when things are at their worst? The Apostle Paul has a fascinating way of challenging the Ephesian Christians to be their best. He says: "Take up God's armour; then you will be able to stand your ground when things are at their worst" (6:13, NEB). That is the great test of maturity—how you take the loss of a mate, or the recurring cancer, or the failure of the "ole ticker," or even the imminent possibility of your own death. How you cope when things are at their worst.

4. Do you know how to enjoy the enjoyable? This changes for each of us at different periods in our lives. For example, at some point in our lives, sex becomes important to us as a prime enjoyable experience. Fishing, golf, needlepoint, the forty-four domino game, symphonies, or growing African violets—any of these might provide enjoyment from time to time. A charismatic experience may even be the top experience of our lives. Here is the point I want to emphasize: authentic living for all of us means that we find things to enjoy and have the creativity and courage to enjoy them.

5. What do you select to attend to? People who get bitter, "sourcasted" one of my rustic friends used to call it, are that way because they focus on the bad aspects of life. They look out the window at a rose garden but end up focusing on the fly specks on the window pane. They have regular "pity parties," feeling sorry for the blows people and life have dealt them. All the while they are looking at the bad things of life, they are overlooking those aspects which evoke gratitude and joy. Selective attention is one of the blessings of God. What we choose to attend to will blight us or bless us, break us or make us, slow us down or grow us like the lily (Matt. 6:28).

6. Do you get more satisfaction out of giving than of

receiving? When we come into this world we spend the
first years saying, "Gimme." Then on our road to autonomy we go through a period of saying, "Leave me alone."
From this we emerge into a "Put out" period, whether
we like it or not. In the middle years most of us begin
to get self-indulgent, "I want my part" period. If we really
mature we come into a joyful period of saying, "I want
my part, but I would like to help you get yours"—the
sane, balanced, equalization period. There is great satisfaction in the "let me help you" period.

In their move toward their potential, many grandparents
progress into a "Let-me-help-you" period without self-in-
fliction, without self-pity, without expectation of gratitude.
What an example to their offspring and to their offspring's
offspring!

LET'S LEAVE A GOOD INHERITANCE

The best estate grandparents can leave to their children
is what they, the children, grandchildren, and even great-
grandchildren, carry around in their memories. We may
even stalk around in their dreams.

I have heard hundreds of people mention their parents
or grandparents, sometimes casually and incidentally, in
the course of their recounting (for therapeutic purposes)
what had influenced them in their lives. Some were left
land, stocks, trusts, or heirlooms. Usually they are grateful,
after a fashion. Most used their material gifts and legacies
rather well.

However, the moving and deeply significant remarks I
have heard, and the eyes that I have seen sparkle with
joy or glisten with well-remembered sadness, have been
about the kind of person a grandmother or a grandfather
was. The satisfaction and inspiration of what "my Granny"
was like or the admiration of a "Grandpa Jones" who lives

on in the grandchild's own character is something to behold.

No doubt such heritages are like the surprises described by Jesus in his delineation of what the Judgment Day will be like. The righteous are taken aback when the Lord says that they had fed him when he was hungry, given him drink when he was thirsty, welcomed him, ministered to him when he was sick, and even visited him when in prison. So might it be with our grandchildren.

Afterword

WRITERS WRITE FOR fame, to be read and reread and remembered. We build monuments to ourselves, leave legacies to institutions, and erect elaborate tombstones to insure that we will not be forgotten or thought to be a nobody.

Especially, and universally, we wish to prolong ourselves in our children, a kind of social immortality. The marvelous genes we have will live on in these distinctive creatures we have spawned. No matter how efficient we become at controlling our own reproduction, we will always pursue this method of achieving immortality that helps console us when we "have fears that we may cease to be" (Keats).

One of my favorite authors, Miguel de Unamuno, seems to come to the heart of the matter in *The Tragic Sense of Life.* Our basic longing, he says, is to be forever. This "hunger for immortality," one of his chapter titles, is what we all secretly work and long for from infancy to the mortuary, whether we are aware of it or not, or even when we deny it most vehemently, or ignore it as placidly as we can.

We want our genes to continue, but a deeper impulse is the desire to continue in the hearts and minds of those we love. We want our children and grandchildren to remember us with a smile on their faces and affection in their hearts.

It was not uncommon in the Old Testament for God's prophets to warn against the sins of fathers' being visited on their children's children—grandparents were important

135

for good or ill. Our actions can be a blessing to our grand-children or a burden for them to overcome.

One burden that a child or grandchild might suffer is grandparents who won't let go—who won't treat grown children as adults. How much better to be remembered as the wise parent who gently, but surely nudged his off-spring out of the nest and into self-sufficiency!

No one wants to be remembered as the grandparent who made an ordeal out of holidays with nagging and petty jealousy nor as one who caused arguments over rules of behavior that conflicted with the young parents'.

No wonder the Bible praises the good woman, that "her children rise up and call her blessed" (Prov. 31:38). And on the male side, "Grandchildren are the crown of old age, and sons are proud of their fathers" (Prov. 17:6, NEB). In the Apostle Paul's first letter to Timothy there is a quaintly tender touch about his learning his sincere faith from his grandmother, Lois, and his mother, Eunice (2 Tim. 1:5).

We can be like these praiseworthy parents if we direct our actions with good common sense—an uncommon thing these days! We can refrain from offering unwanted advice; we can build respect for authority by deferring to the young parents' household rules; we can work to build the self-esteem of children and grandchildren, to give them enough confidence to succeed.

Our reward will be more than praise—it will also be love. What is love between family members? It is caring what happens to another and doing something about it. It is reaching out to another human being. It is encourag-ing the downhearted. It is drawing near. Love is really the warm acceptance of another person as he/she is. And that is difficult!

Call it *agape* (the New Testament word for God's kind of love), mature love, friendship, or whatever. One factor must be present: contact, getting in touch. Love is never at a distance—neither God's love nor man's.

Getting the family together and keeping in touch will require patience, restraint, generosity, and humor. But that's a small price to pay to be remembered with love.